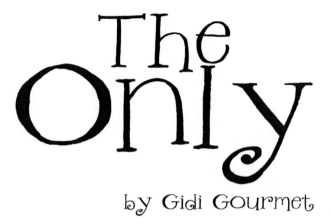

The Only

by Gidi Gourmet

Gideon Hirtenstein,
Executive Chef

authorHOUSE®

AuthorHouse™
1663 Liberty Drive
Bloomington, IN 47403
www.authorhouse.com
Phone: 1 (800) 839-8640

Published by AuthorHouse 11/05/2016

ISBN: 978-1-5246-4867-1 (sc)
ISBN: 978-1-5246-4865-7 (hc)
ISBN: 978-1-5246-4866-4 (e)

Library of Congress Control Number: 2016918642

Print information available on the last page.

Any people depicted in stock imagery provided by Thinkstock are models, and such images are being used for illustrative purposes only. Certain stock imagery © Thinkstock.

This book is printed on acid-free paper.

The Only Source by Gidi Gourmet
Catering 80-100 people for under $1,000.
Printed in the USA 2016
Book by Gideon Hirtenstein
Executive chef - 47 years of experience
Graduated in 1969 - European-trained
Designed by Gideon Hirtenstein

The Book Topics
Catering 80-100 people for under $1,000.00
Individuals in the catering and restaurant business.
Ideas for free decorations.
Information for the consumer.
Information about your event coordinator, disc jockey, photographer, and insurance.
Ideas for consumers to save money.
Health department regulations directly related to the food business.

Thank you to Nicole Hirtenstein

Contents

Introduction

As an executive chef for the first fifteen years of my career, both overseas and in the United States, I learned firsthand how to properly manage and train kitchen employees and staff to ensure a successful business and a harmonious work environment. When you own your own business, you must overcome many unique challenges—employee issues; industry-specific dilemmas; concerns with quality and presentation; and finances, including cost, labor, and insurance expenditures—in order to keep everything running as smoothly as possible while maintaining strict regulatory compliance.

A great many business owners try to avoid or ignore the considerable challenges every business must invariably face. When you consciously avoid these problems, they eventually catch up with you in greater magnitude, often when it is too late to reverse, rectify, or resolve them successfully and inexpensively. Throughout my career as owner and executive chef of Gidi Gourmet LLC, I have seen many new caterers come and go. The rapid demise of these businesses was not surprising; the owners clearly lacked a proper foundation in the culinary field and were shortsighted and self-destructive in their business practices.

Only about 10 percent of individuals who start a catering business have the experience in the field, professional training, and education credentials they need to be successful. Even those who have extensive training and impressive culinary backgrounds still need to properly handle the many unexpected challenges that come along before they can earn a reputation built on uncompromisingly high standards and quality. Many fledgling caterers have little or no experience to guide them and must resort to hiring an expensive professional chef. When you start a business this way, you immediately put yourself at a disadvantage, both financially and professionally.

A lack of requisite knowledge and experience with specific aspects of the catering and restaurant business will increase your chances of getting trapped. The excitement of individuals eager to enter the food-service business can exceed realistic expectations. Too often, they are only focused on the positive and rewarding aspects of the business and how quickly they can earn a large profit. They forget how much energy and risk is involved, not to mention the substantial financial investment necessary not only to stay afloat but also to achieve long-term success.

Many small-business owners irreparably harm themselves and their business by getting involved with high levels of financing, exhausting all available sources of money. They collateralize their homes and cars, borrow from credit cards, and drain any accessible sources of credit in order to start and sustain their businesses. This perilous maneuvering effectively puts their families and their life savings in jeopardy with uncertain, high-risk undertakings. This is a recipe for failure personally and professionally, and it can easily lead to bankruptcy and the prospect of having to start all over again to rebuild and reacquire what was lost.

Do not fall into this trap by allowing the excitement of your endeavor to take you above and beyond the reach of reality. It is imperative that you lay out all the details—from small to large—and anticipate with sound solutions the challenges you expect to encounter. You must calculate these obstacles from the very start with realistic expectations and outcomes. If you must convince and persuade yourself with unrealistic motivations and contingencies, it is possible that you will not achieve the results you seek.

If you are a business owner and decide to hire a professional chef, you must establish that the chef is not only competent but highly capable in performing a variety of tasks in order to ensure the business is successful. The following are some basic areas to cover in an interview to hire a professional chef:

- credentials—culinary education and professional accomplishments
- prior employers and positions held
- experience and knowledge with calculating food cost
- ability to keep costs low
- ability to control labor cost

- creative ability
- ability to put menus together for different seasons
- ability to perform scheduling
- willingness to work as many hours as needed
- familiarity with all sections of the kitchen
- ability to work with other people
- ability to hold weekly meetings
- willingness to wash pots and pans if necessary
- ability to treat the employees under him or her with respect
- ability to take the word *no* from the owner or management above him or her
- legal status—clean record with no violations
- willingness to maintain the kitchen to the high standards required by the health department, including city and county regulations
- if not a culinary school graduate, willingness to be a working chef with the title of "executive chef"
- willingness to perform the duty of all positions in the kitchen at any time necessary
- ability to mentor and train staff to a higher level

For many business owners, it seems easier to bestow upon a small-time cook the venerable title of executive chef. It is much more convenient and easy to make a name tag for a couple of dollars and pretend you have a quality chef in the kitchen. The tag may be inexpensive, but the price you're going to pay every month because of inexperience will inevitably cost you and your business a great deal more. You are effectively destroying your business when you hire somebody who isn't capable of holding the kitchen and staff to the necessary standards required to keep your business comfortably afloat while generating a profit.

It may seem more practical and less expensive to hire unqualified kitchen workers, but those who do so will eventually face harsh reality. Despite apparent savings at the beginning, by the end of the month, many thousands of dollars will be lost to the labor inefficiencies of unqualified workers. When you hire inexperienced workers, productivity and quality usually decrease. One common result of unqualified staff is overordering and eventual waste of food supplies. This predicament leads to unnecessary food loss and increased labor costs. Overordering food that ends up in the garbage and high labor costs are both important factors to control, as they can quite easily put you out of business.

It is not uncommon for business owners to promote dishwashers to run their kitchen operations. Although some owners may disagree, this is a huge mistake, as the overall quality of the kitchen and business suffers when an untrained, low-skilled person is put in charge of even seemingly simple matters in the kitchen. The result is invariably a lower class of food quality and aesthetic presentation and an environment of low productivity and lack of attention to proper sanitation. You can't expect someone who is not familiar with the big picture of food services to run a successful kitchen operation.

When you run a food business of almost any kind, you must operate with a high level of consistency from day one in everything you do. If your employees in the kitchen work for low wages, you can expect to get low-quality food and both sloppy and inconsistent presentation. As a business owner in food services, you have to ensure a few very important things from the beginning. Start by creating rules for all staff in your operation to follow. Your rules might include the following:

1. Kitchen workers must be clean and wear uniforms: white jacket and checkered pants.
2. Long fingernails are not allowed.
3. Men must be shaved.
4. Chef hats are mandatory.
5. No bandannas are allowed.
6. No baseball caps are allowed.
7. Girls in the kitchen may wear hairnets.
8. No watches or jewelry are allowed during work because they trap bacteria.
9. Kitchen workers must be wear appropriate black shoes with grip on the bottom.
10. All staff must wear name and position tags.
11. The bathroom in the kitchen must be sanitary at all times and cleaned twice a day by the dishwasher.
12. The floor must have rubber mats.

13. The drain line in the kitchen must be cleaned with bleach twice a week.

14. Kitchen trash cans must daily be washed outside, sprayed with sanitizer, and lined with a trash bag before being brought back into the kitchen.

15. The hand-washing sink must have disposable paper towels and sanitizing hand wash. All employees must wash hands before leaving the bathroom.

16. The back door must have a screen at all times.

17. The hood system must be cleaned once a week; the stove and oven must be scrubbed once a week.

18. All pots and pans must be washed every day so grease will not burn or cause a fire.

19. Before leaving the kitchen for the day, all kitchen personnel must mop the floors and clean the entire kitchen so that it is ready for the next day's morning shift.

20. All prepared food, sauces, and soups stored in refrigeration must be labeled with content and the date and time they were cooked.

21. Any new products must be put on a separate shelf or in a separate side of the walk-in or reach-in refrigeration.

22. All frozen meat must be received frozen and put immediately into the storage freezer.

23. Dry food must be stored at least ten inches above the ground and organized properly on stainless-steel shelving.

24. No wood products may be used for storage; built-up wood structures within the refrigeration facility are not allowed.

25. Have an exterminator come once a month to spray during off hours.

26. Do not use any chemicals for washing floors or the pots and pans. It is not permitted by the health department.

27. You must have thermometers in all refrigeration and freezers.

28. You must have a meter apparatus for measuring hot and cold temperatures at all times in the kitchen.

29. All kitchen personnel must work with white aprons.

30. No phone usage during working hours.

31. It is mandatory to not have any cups in the kitchen or on the working table.

32. You must hose down the rubber kitchen mats outside the door and scrub them with a heavy scrubber with gloves on.

33. You must have a photo album readily available with all of the dishes on the menu in the event that there is a question or need to explain and describe preparation and presentation.

34. Avoid receiving any food deliveries during lunch or dinner hours. The reason is that you cannot confirm whether the frozen products were delivered appropriately and frozen, and you cannot check if the fresh products were delivered in good condition and the quantity you ordered has been delivered. A major issue is that you may not have the time to put the products away properly and organize them correctly.

35. You cannot take a break during the service time.

36. You cannot take a smoking break when you wish. Only five-minute breaks every hour are allowed.

37. In the event that you have a problem with an employee, you must have a formal sheet prepared to record any employee transgressions. The form should be signed by the employee, indicating his or her understanding and compliance with your policy that you are willing to accommodate up to "two strikes." The third strike will result in termination.

38. Any time you need to confirm or confront a problem or issue with an employee, you must have another manager present in the office as a witness to the conversation.

39. If a male supervisor needs to confront a female employee, it is preferable to have an assistant female manager present in the office with the door left open.

40. Never invite a female employee to your office for any subject or reason whatsoever, and vice versa for a female supervisor.

41. You have the right to record all conversations with the full knowledge and approval of the party invited to the conversation. The individual must be explicitly told the conversation will be recorded and his or her voice must consent to it on the recording.

42. If at any time you see conflict between employees in any area at work, you must take charge, talk to each individual, and get to the bottom of the problem. You must have an open meeting so everybody can speak out, and then you can make the final decision on how to fix the problem.

43. Avoid having family members working together. Many difficulties and conflicts can erupt between workers, especially when it involves workers and relatives.

44. You should not have a boyfriend and girlfriend working together— at the bar, in the kitchen, or as waitstaff. That is, in no positions at all.

The Consumer

How to Save Money for Your Next Event
and What You Should Look For

Throughout my forty-five year career, I have learned many different ways of saving money while achieving a high-quality presentation for a variety of celebrations and affairs. In this section, you'll find a variety of ideas for saving money, providing for your guests, and ensuring high-quality food and presentation at your next event. Over the years, it has become evident to me how difficult it is for people to spend large amounts of money on their celebration. This has made it clear to me what people are really looking for and how to fulfill their wishes.

I've also noticed a variety of shows on TV that may be harmful to your expectations. It can be very confusing to watch these shows. The ideas presented do not fit the budget of the majority of the audience. The shows typically do not relate to what the average person can afford, and they are likely very far removed from any realistic budget. Don't plan some sort of fantasy affair; it can be very costly and put you in debt. My suggestion is to live in reality and consider what is affordable for you.

At the same time, you have to understand that caterers cannot work for free. They can negotiate with you a little, but good caterers are not drive-throughs or brown-baggers. Before you try to bargain, go to a drive-through, buy a couple of items, and see what you get. At that point, you might start thinking more reasonably. You may be able to bargain with some low-class caterers, which I consider the meatball and chicken-wing caterers. Don't compare the first-class caterer to a third-class caterer. When you hire a good caterer, you will get good food, nicer equipment, better presentation, and people who act like professionals.

Be aware that when caterers advertise they have been many years in the business, you must really check how long the current owners have been involved. Some businesses, after many years, have been sold to somebody else who might use the reputation but has no clue how to run the business. You also have to look out for people who decide overnight they want to start a catering business, and they work from their home. It is illegal to work this way, without a health-department permit. This is the only permit they can operate with, and of course after this comes a business license and liability insurance.

Before you hire a catering company, make your own investigation as to which caterer is going to be best for you and your budget. Many caterers are setting up their friends and family to post favorable comments and give them all kinds of titles to look good. This is exactly what you don't want to base your decision on. Before you hire a caterer for your next event, you will want to look for, consider, and ask about the following:

1. The caterer should have a current and updated health-department permit; license for the county and/or city; and liability insurance.

2. Find out the credentials of potential caterers; their background; whether they have a degree from an accredited culinary institute and which one; and the number of years they've been in food services.

3. Request a minimum of five catering references from the past twelve months.

4. Gather proposals from at least four different catering companies before making a decision.

5. Request full menus with everything included, such as setup, cleanup, and waitressing. The company letterhead must state the number of hours and anything else the caterer agrees to provide, so there are no questions or discrepancies with the service and costs expected.

6. Request that all prospective companies invite you to an event they are catering, so that you can make a comparison and reach a final decision.

7. Ask the caterer to provide china, silver, glass, updated chafing dishes, skirting, covers, and nondisposables.

8. Make sure the price you are quoted you is inclusive of all fees, waitstaff, and tax, with no exceptions or extras.

9. Make sure the waitstaff wears black and white uniforms with a tie and black shoes. No other colors permitted. No exception for sport shoes or any other style.

10. Ask whether each caterer has a dedicated manager to oversee the catering matters.

11. Request that members of the waitstaff make no phone calls during the reception.

12. Be sure you have a valid license to operate a bar if you are using the caterer to staff the bar.

13. When you decide to sign a contract, make sure everything you discussed verbally with the caterer is in the contract with complete details. Look out for provisional loopholes that can increase the price of the agreement you made.

14. When you sign the contract and put a deposit down, ensure that the contract stipulates that the caterer has some sort of security in case there is a mishap. At the same time, caterers have to secure themselves in case you decide for some reason to back off from the contract. There will be some penalties here.

15. If you decide to use a banquet hall, you must inspect and assess the inside of the hall to see how it looks and what kind of tables and chairs it is outfitted with. Determine whether the furniture is old or broken, the lighting is poor or excessive, the rooms are dated or dirty, or the decorations are tacky or lacking. You will also want to see if there is a kitchen or pantry in the back as well as refrigerators, freezers, and a stove. Commercial-grade equipment may not be necessary; very basic equipment is generally adequate and acceptable.

16. Notice if the banquet hall uses silk flowers and plants, as this is unacceptable. They collect dust, and they are not sanitary—better for use in a funeral home.

17. Make a point to use the bathroom during your visit to a banquet hall. Keep your eyes open to see if it's clean. Use your own

judgment. See if anything is broken, and if the facilities are comfortable to use.

18. Take photographs of any damage you see at the banquet hall. Most have damage provisions in their contracts, and they will come after you at will. Photographic proof with date and time stamps will protect you from any potential liability.

19. When dealing with a caterer or banquet hall, be clear that any waiters or waitresses with tattoos on their arms must diligently cover them up with long sleeves.

20. Never use a microwave in the kitchen. Use only a stove, oven, broiler, grill, etc.

21. Before you commit to any contract with a client, you must go to the location you're going to cater and look at it carefully. Determine whether you have direct access to the building, if there is an appropriate loading dock or parking next to the building, and any other unexpected scenarios that may come up. If it's outside, you'll need to ensure that there is water and electrical access for your catering area.

22. If the catering area is outdoors, check the ground to see if it's soft; tables and chairs may sink in, making it impossible to set up the seating. In addition, you must make sure the buffet table legs sit on a hard surface; otherwise it may collapse when heavy items are placed on top of it. Ensure that table covers do not go all the way down to the ground.

23. If you don't have the appropriate access or requirements to cater properly, you must consider charging more money for any help, labor, or other expenses that are necessary to address any deficiencies.

24. I highly recommend using of stainless steel or heavy aluminum equipment in the kitchen. Teflon products are not recommended for commercial use because of the risk of coating removal during the cleaning process or toxic fumes released from overheating.

25. When creating a menu, try to devise a menu with items your competitor does not have offer.

26. If you aspire to be an upscale caterer with high-quality fare, stay away from meatballs, chicken wings, biscuits, and other basic menu items.

27. Implement a policy restricting friends of employees in the workplace, and prohibit breaks to see visiting friends.

28. Many chefs and owners seem to lack an understanding that they must perform a diligent inventory of all food and products related to the kitchen every week. This is an essential and mandatory practice to control food cost and should be performed weekly with no excuses.

29. When performing inventory duties, you must have a commercial-grade scale available and a special sheet that specifies and documents each item you use in your kitchen.

30. In order to ensure accuracy while performing inventory duties, it is preferable to have one person inventory while another writes.

31. Do not carry high inventory of any kind of product. The money spent on high inventory that expires will, at some point, be wasted.

32. Try to control or restrict your purchasing habits to twice a week so that all of your items are as fresh as possible. You can control your food cost and inventory in the most efficient, money-saving way.

33. When you compile your purchase order, methodically go through the kitchen, refrigeration, walk-ins, freezer, and dry storage units to determine replenishment levels.

34. Some items in the dry storage do not need to be ordered twice a week and can be safely ordered on a biweekly basis.

35. Make sure you are uninterrupted during your purchase-order duties to avoid any oversights or mistakes.

36. The communication between the morning and evening shift must be worked out every day upon crew transition. It is important that everything related to the operation be documented in writing and given to the person taking over in the kitchen or any other department. Without some form of written documentation, people can claim whatever they want. The only one who's going to get hurt in these situations is the incoming shift—and of course, the business itself. As the owner or executive chef, it is your duty to communicate to your staff to the best of your knowledge.

37. Watch your labor costs. Add up the budget worksheet on a daily basis, including all purchasing and labor costs, to avoid incurring any overtime on your payroll.

38. You as a chef or owner must be present anytime there is an emergency or you are shorthanded. Your salary structure is totally different from the rest of the staff. That's what is required for management positions. No excuses.

39. As the chef, if you see that certain things are not going right—related to the food and presentation, or any other chaos in the kitchen—you must speak to the owner and/or general manager to address these concerns before they get out of hand. Every business owner, from small to large, should be happy to discuss all concerns related to a business enterprise. An owner who does not want to listen to obvious issues will face more serious problems at some point.

40. There are many business owners in the catering field with no knowledge of what it takes to properly run a food operation. A disproportionate number are ignorant and foolhardy in their operations. They refuse to listen or learn, as their huge ego leaves them believing they are too good to be serious about their business. These owners do not last long in the business and eventually disappear from the landscape.

41. Many owners have good credit and feel comfortable, and so they ignore their business needs. They do not want to invest their own personal energy into the business. They think that if they supply the financing, they don't have to go beyond that and oversee it. They think they can play golf or sit in a spa somewhere and everything will run by itself. This is the reason many companies go out of business.

42. If you're a chef or manager facing a hardheaded business owner, try to sit down and explain all the downsides carefully. Many owners will try to interfere with the menu choices as well as the entire kitchen staff. This is a bad situation to get into.

43. Your responsibility as a chef requires you to lay out the catering menu to accommodate different seasons and the demographic tastes and sensibilities of the local geographic area. Make it your goal as a chef to incorporate, as much as feasible, fresh products like meat, poultry, seafood, vegetables, and fruits into your menu. Keep this in mind when you compile food orders twice a week.

44. Do not make a large menu. They are expensive to keep. You should have an adequate selection for your clientele, but one that is appropriately and sensibly limited. Large menus can cause havoc for your restaurant or catering business because you cannot reasonably keep up with excessive items on the menu. You are going to reach a point pretty quickly where the items will gets stale, expire, or even become poisonous.

45. If there is a fundamental lack of understanding between you and the owner in reference to the meal and how to run the kitchen, it is obvious you have come to a sticking point. You as a chef must make a decision as to whether you can deal with someone you cannot work with productively in good faith.

46. You must maintain strict organization within your kitchen, coolers, and walk-ins, and stay on top of it on a daily basis. If you're unable to, you must assign the sous chef to handle it properly.

47. As an executive chef, you should only use olive oil and real butter. The quality of your food will be vastly improved.

48. As a business or individual owner, you likely borrowed the money for capital and collateralized your home, stocks, or some other assets you own. You may have also borrowed from credit cards to meet financial obligations. If something happens to you, what will happen to all the collateral and commitments you have assumed? You must be very careful not to jeopardize your family's lifestyle and well-being because you didn't plan to protect them from your business mistakes. It is wise to form your business as a limited liability corporation to protect your personal and family assets.

49. As an owner, you should have cameras on the exterior of your building, and especially in the interior areas where the cash registers are located. You will be more comfortable with these precautions in place. If you find out something is askew, you can handle it more confidently knowing you have recorded documentation.

50. Owners must make it a high priority to keep tax liabilities in order and paid on time. Failure to adhere to this rule will catch up with you and can potentially cause you to lose your business.

51. At least three seasons out of the year you can use dry leaves, weeds, branches, and bamboo as decorations. You can also place

a combination of green leaves in between them. The greenery will go all year long and complement any other colors.

52. Holly branches work well in the fall and winter, and you can lay them on a table or in a vase. Just don't set them next to the food.

53. Spray-paint corn husks with a color of your choice, or leave them natural. Use them as you did the bamboo above.

54. Place candles inside of hanging glass candleholders and hang in the center of each table or as decoration in or around tents or buildings.

55. Purchase small copper watering cans at a gardening store. Put one in the center of each table. Take four or five rocks and put them around each watering can. Fill the watering can with weeds, flowers, greenery, or whatever you choose.

56. Wash a bundle of oyster and clam shells really well with bleach. Put a touch of glue around the edges of a piece of hard cardboard about seven to eight inches wide. Cover the glue with a layer of mixed shells, putting a little glue on the back of the shells as well. Leave a hole in the center. Fit a little clay or glass bowl in the hole and fill it with a little sand. Take a mini cactus or any small plant you choose and put it in the bowl for a nice centerpiece.

57. Wash and dry old wine bottles and glue little rocks or beach glass to them. Stick a long candle of your color choice in the bottle.

58. Cut a pineapple in half lengthwise with the leaves still on. Take small skewers tipped with strawberries or berries and stick them into the pineapple half.

59. Cut a small watermelon in a zigzag all the way around. Clean out the inside and fill the rind with fresh fruit, like a basket. Put on a heavy disposable plate and arrange magnolia leaves or any other greenery all around.

60. If the event will be in a backyard or attached to a house, buy a commercially available six-by-fifteen-foot bamboo fence that is already rolled up and use it as a temporary privacy fence.

61. Designate the area for your party event by lining it with barrels full of plants.

62. During the Christmas season, use fresh miniature pine trees for centerpieces. Tie them up with bows and place rocks and mini

red tea-light candles around them. You can wrap them up in little Christmas lights too.

63. For the area where the reception will be, use any pine tree in different sections, decorated with lights. Live trees are preferable and are really cheap. Place the bottom of each tree in a bucket when the event is finished, and when you have the time you can put it back in the ground so you do not waste money.

64. Put a tree branch with an apple still on it into a long vase. Use sand or rocks to hold it in place. You can do the same thing with pears, peaches, or other fruit.

65. Put thick marsh grass into a vase or clay—or take a PVC pipe, cut it about twelve inches in height, put it on the table, and surround it with five rocks, sticking the marsh grass inside of it. You can spray-paint the pipe a couple of weeks before with the color you choose for your centerpiece.

66. Fill up a vase, clay pot, or any other kind of holder you can get that's cheap with medium-sized red-tipped branches. Make sure the sticks are uneven sizes.

67. You as a consumer must be careful, because some individuals advertise and promote themselves as chef consultants. Be sure to ask questions about their credentials and qualifications as a consultant, including the following:
    - Where did you last work? In what position?
    - What's your education and knowledge directly related to food service?
    - How much experience do you have?
    - Do you have a minimum of five recent references where you worked as a consultant?
    - What duties do you expect to perform as a consultant?
    - Do you have pictures of the variety of work you've done?
    - Will you be able to handle the entire event?
    - Do you have any cooking-related knowledge?
    - Have you ever been in an executive position related to the food business?
    - How long have you worked as a private consultant?

68. In most cases, people do not use consultants, and if they do, the consultant has full knowledge about coordinating an event. Consultants must be able to take most of the load off you. You as the caterer should have a lengthy conversation with any individuals who represent themselves as a consultant or coordinator. The questions asked should provide some evidence and reference as to their credentials, and you will be able to determine if they are qualified to handle the job. Some people are excellent with verbal communication and present themselves well, but when it comes down to the actual work, they are very far from the expectations they portrayed. If you decide to hire this type of individual, do not make any immediate or rushed decisions. Look into the evidence which he or she presents to you, call some references, and make an informed decision.

Money-Saving Ideas for Consumers

Most people try to save money when planning their event. This is natural for all of us. I will provide you with many ideas on how to save money from the beginning and be on top of it 100 percent. Some of the ideas are going to seem unrealistic or funny, but they are all possible. If you have a lot of money, then these ideas are not for you. But if you are running tight with money and still want to have a nice event, read carefully.

After many years in the catering business, serving a high volume of guests at a variety of different events, I have come to the conclusion that if it is not a large event, you can basically do it all on your own. If it is a high-volume event, you will probably need to be equipped with storage, equipment, preparation area, and more. For small events, though—anything between fifty and one hundred people—you can plan and execute everything with very little expense, and without hiring a caterer.

If you do your own catering, plan for everything to be spontaneous and down-to-earth. Don't try to go too fancy, or you may blow up your Visa and MasterCard and end up spending more than you would have if you'd hired a caterer. Start by laying out a budget. This should include all expenses from beginning to end, with no surprises. When you have these ideas, you can start to lay out your plan.

My recommendation to those who decide to do their own catering is to start planning between six and eight months ahead. The following are some considerations for your planning:

1. Start by determining how many people you will invite to your event.

2. If you are going to host the event in your backyard, you will need to make sure you can accommodate the number of people you're inviting.

3. If the food will be served buffet-style with a seated area, make sure you have enough space for tables, chairs, buffet station, drink station, and bar, if you have one.

4. To save a lot of hassle and many inconveniences as far as chairs, tables, and table covers go, do a stand-up cocktail and hors d'oeuvre party. This will be much more convenient for both you and your guests. People can move around better if it's a cocktail party with hors d'oeuvres. They can mobilize themselves better, and in many cases it's much more convenient and attractive.

5. Remember that your guests will not expect common and standard food selections. They will likely anticipate and appreciate more upscale, exciting, and exotic fare. Give them something to talk about and remember.

6. When you host your party in the backyard, you have the advantage of natural decorations surrounding you, so you don't have to spend money for flowers and other greenery. Take the plants, bushes, flowers, and any wooden benches you have and stage them in the area where you are going to all get together.

7. Instead of renting a tent, make your own canopy to fit seventy-five to one hundred people. It is all natural, looks good, and is safe.

8. In the backyard, you will have easy access to water, electricity, and the kitchen. You also have the option of an open grill.

9. To cater your own event, you will need the following items: approximately three large coolers, a home-style oven, a home-style grill, two preparation tables to work with, and some ice.

10. You can have an open bar and use all disposable plates, forks, and utensils. In this type of event, you will only need a couple of friends or family members to cover all of your needs.

11. All the products you need should be already purchased two days prior to the event. In some cases, depending on the menu and type of meat you use, you can prepare food a week or two beforehand and freeze it.

12. When you do your own catering, you have to lay out exactly what you want to have without changes, because changes can be costly—and of course, storage-wise, you might face a problem if you are not prepared for it.

13. After you prep the food, it must all be kept in the refrigerator. If you don't have an extra refrigerator at home, you can put the food in coolers with bags of ice placed underneath. Be very careful to keep consistent temperatures in the cooler and refrigeration. Do not open the coolers too many times so the temperature can stay as steady as possible. All the prepared food must be wrapped up really well in aluminum foil.

14. The drawback to catering your own party is that you will need to be more involved and deal with minor issues normally left to the caterer. Compile an exact list of the items you need to purchase for the menu. All the ingredients must be in the house so you won't have to run to the store. This can cause an inconvenience and disrupt other things you need to do.

15. If you decide to cater your own event, shop online and buy brand-new table covers if you need them. You can buy them by the dozen; they are nylon and cost approximately eight dollars each. They're actually cheaper to rent, but if you decide to buy them, you can always resell them for half price after the event.

16. If instead of using your backyard you choose to rent a banquet hall, it can cost you between $800 and $1,000 for a four- to six-hour rental period. You will also need to be concerned with liability issues for the place you're renting. Some places may want you to have extra insurance to compensate them. This insurance can cost you between $400 and $600. Without it, the banquet hall will not rent its facilities to you.

17. The above is just the rental and insurance expense for the banquet hall; it's already very costly and you haven't done anything else yet. You will have additional expenses to consider, such as disc jockey,

photographer, catering company, florist, wedding cake, invitation cards, bar, license for alcohol, and more.

18. You must lay out all the expenses. If you're really diligent in your research, you can probably get a better deal from different companies that are less expensive, which will factor positively into your budget. Do not commit to something you cannot afford. If you use different companies, pay as much up front as you can. This will make it much easier to not pay in chunks when the time comes.

19. If you have an outage of electricity and no gas available, you can make yourself a fire pit for your entire dinner. Make your pit eighty-four inches long by thirty-six inches wide by twenty-four inches deep. Dig the hole and make it as level as you can. Put cinderblocks (eight-by-eight-by-sixteen) across the hole and fill the holes of the cinderblocks with sand. Spread pieces of chopped logs all around the hole.

    Before you use the fire pit, you must light all the wood on fire and cover it up with a long aluminum pan approximately an hour and a half before you use it. You can put your entire menu in separate aluminum pans on top of the blocks, one next to the other. Depending on the menu, you can start with meat and poultry. These will be the first to go into the pit, followed by other items that do not need to be in the pit for a long time. It all depends on the menu.

    Remember, since you are very limited on equipment and you don't have thermal hot boxes for the food, you will use a regular long-sided cooler. Put clean towels on the bottom of the cooler. As soon as anything comes out of the oven, wrap it up immediately with plastic wrap and foil, stick it into the cooler as quickly as you can, and cover the top with another clean towel to preserve the heat. From the cooler, put the food into the chafing dishes.

20. The following are ideas for inexpensive decorations for your event.

21. Place mini pine tree branches in a vase or lay them over the center of the tables, surrounded by some yellowish rocks. Holly branches can also be placed into a vase or clay pot or laid in the center of the table.

22. Tie about six or seven bamboo sticks (with leaves, if possible) together with string, thicker side down. The height should be about twelve inches. Stick flowers of your choice into the top of the bamboo.

23. Place two or three real sunflowers into an inexpensive medium-size vase purchased at a discount store.

24. Place fresh corn in the husk in the center of the table. Lay four or five on top of each other in a circular pattern or design, leaving space in the middle for small candles. This arrangement should only cost about two dollars per table. You can find corn cheap at the farmer's market.

25. For each table, take a pack of sprouts, fluff them up a little, and put them in a six-inch inch clay pot bottom in the center of the table. Stick a ten-inch candle of your color choice in the center.

26. Stand up pinecones still on the stick in a thin vase. Paint the pinecones with the color of your choice or just leave them natural. You can paint the vase a color of your choice as well.

27. Use wildflowers depending on the season. Azalea push sticks or any evergreen sticks work well too. Lay them in the center of the table or place them in clay pots.

28. Use branches from evergreen bushes to tie up every corner in the area.

29. Take some long bamboo sticks and tie them to any free or open space you find in the banquet area.

30. Cut logs into round disc plates and lay them in the center of each table, placing rocks on top. Place some candles of your choice in the center of the table. A single bag of tea lights will cover at least fifteen tables and only set you back four dollars or so. You can cut the logs yourself if you have the tools available.

31. Place fresh fruit-tree branches into a vase and add some gravel on top. Use mini limes or any other hard fruit.

32. Stick grapevines (with leaves attached) in a mini clay pot about six inches tall. In the center of the leaves, place real red or green grapes to complete the decoration.

33. Purchase an oval or round mini basket about six to eight inches wide. Pad the basket with some green leaves and pile in fresh

strawberries with the leaves still attached. You can also spread individual leaves around the basket.

34. Fill a basket or mini eight-inch clay pot with peaches and fresh fruit. Place pine needles under it.

35. Fill a six- to eight-inch clay pot with items that fit the season.

36. Fill a six- to eight-inch glass bowl (like a fishbowl) with inexpensive rocks and weeds. Add the weeds just before the event and drop in some glow-in-the-dark stones.

37. Fill a tall vase with three or four different colors of sand. Use the ambient colors of the wedding or event. Place fresh flowers with stems into the sand.

38. Stick a tall candle in a medium candleholder. Add some rocks around the glass.

39. Wrap a colored ribbon of your choice around a medium-size vase. Put it on a colored runner down the middle of the table.

40. Set fresh geraniums (small or medium) on top of a flat circular piece of cut log and surround it with fresh flower petals.

41. Take a small basket and fill it up with gourds and squash.

42. You can also use a basket filled with whole fresh vegetables. Place grape leaves or other leaves on top and around the basket.

43. Carve the top and middle out of mini pumpkins, put a candle inside, and set some rocks in the center.

44. Place fresh spinach leaves or kale and red or green grapes on small cutting boards (approximately one dollar each) and sprinkle with granulated sugar.

45. Pour melted semisweet chocolate with evaporated milk in a mini glass bowl about four to five inches in circumference. Add a little Kahlúa so the mixture stays moist. Place the bowl in the center of the table on top of some green pine needles and place fresh strawberries on skewers around them for dipping.

46. Wrap up a small mini aluminum can with a light bow of your color. Stick it in the center of a bottle of wine or shampoo which will be opened at dinner.

47. Place french bread, assorted cheeses, and some hard salami across a medium-size cutting board.

48. Build a small stone candleholder with larger stones for the bottom and smaller ones as you build upward, gluing them on. Leave a gap in the center for a candle.

49. Lay four pieces of split log at different angles in a concentric circle in the center of the table and place a long candle in the center of them.

50. Use hay bales as an outdoor decoration around a tent and seating area.

51. For the seating area, you can leave a candle for each seated person.

52. Stick mini skewers in an eight-inch Styrofoam cone. Stick pinecones on the skewers. You can wrap the cones with silver or gold foil before you put the skewers in and then station the cones on top of some hay pieces.

53. Place green magnolia branches in the center of the table. Between the leaves, place a tall, thick candle in the color of your choice.

54. Put fresh azalea flower stems in a vase.

55. Carve a mini watermelon into the shape of a basket with a handle. Fill it with a variety of strawberries, blueberries, and blackberries.

56. Carve a honeydew melon and fill it up with fresh cherries (with the stems). Place some green leaves, like spinach, on top of it.

57. Stick skewers tipped with petite rolls into a mini Styrofoam cone.

58. Set an assortment of decorated cupcakes on a split log and place a picture of the bride and groom or other honoree between the cupcakes.

59. To decorate your space outside, strew the area with wavy ribbons of your color choice, which can be mixed in with white ribbons.

60. Stick natural weeds in a long tall vase. Paint the vase any color you want.

61. If you use fresh branches of any kind, they should be cut on the day of your event.

62. Put three or four fresh pomegranates in the center of the table and set up a few rocks and flower petals between them.

63. Place a bunch of tiki torches around the reception area and light them shortly before the guests arrive.

64. Never use bug spray or any other chemicals, as they can be poisonous and dangerous around the food.

65. Put a small basket with wild figs dipped in granulated sugar on top of some fig leaves in the middle of the table.

66. Fill a bowl with gravel and add some food coloring. Let it dry and then transfer the gravel into a decorative bowl.

67. Fill a twenty-two-inch glass vase with rocks or grass. Stick in some natural flowers and weeds, and have a fabric of your color choice hanging off the side from top to bottom.

68. Put the right-sized candles in a decorative candleholder that holds three or four candles.

69. Wash and bleach six or seven clam or oyster shells and set them in the center of the table. Put multicolored tea-light candles in them. Add a few rocks between the shells.

70. Set three large sunflower heads and set in the center of the table on top of a small pile of pine needles.

71. Tie bundles of hay with rope or fabric. Make enough bundles for the tables or for decorations in general.

72. For the guest area, use old barrels, old benches, a swing, or preplanted flowers.

73. Magnolia leaves and branches can be used for your outdoor bungalow. You can use them twelve months a year because they are evergreens and inexpensive. If you are resourceful, you can probably get them for free, and they fit well with many other colors.

74. Tie up several bamboo poles (with leaves, if possible) in a bundle and put torches between them. You can then arrange them in several places around the bungalow or tent. You can also dig a one-foot hole and put a bundle of bamboo inside the hole, filling them with dirt.

75. Instead of a tent, save some money by making your own quick and easy bungalow, which doesn't need a permit or any construction. Pick up a few pieces of lumber: for the side of a bungalow for approximately seventy-five to a hundred guests, you will need twelve pieces of four-by-four-by-ten and sixteen pieces of two-by-four-by-sixteen. You will also need a hammer and some nails. Dig a hole about a foot and a half deep for each stud. After placing the studs into the holes, secure them by filling the gap around the stud

with small pieces of rocks. Cover with dirt packed in really good. There is no need for cement. You then place the two-by-four as a beam on top of it. Use long branches of pine needles to create the roof. If there is a chance of rain, for fifteen to twenty dollars you can buy a large plastic tarp and roll it over the roof area so you don't notice the plastic tarp from inside.

Cover each post with large pieces of pine branches and tie it together with rope. Stick solar lights into each pine-tree post. For the entrance of the bungalow, set up pine branches in a circular pattern. Inside the center of the bungalow, place a small fountain (if you have one) on cinder blocks and cover the blocks with pine branches.

76. For an outdoor party, you can do a bonfire that is six feet by six feet with logs, and you can build it up to approximately seven feet high. It can be prepared seven weeks prior to the reception. You can make a seated area fifteen to twenty feet away from it. Try to keep it in an area where you have immediate water access if necessary. At the end of the night, put water on it until you put the fire out.

77. For your seating area, you can make quick tables from two pieces of wood, twelve by twelve by twelve feet. Put them on top of three layers of cinder blocks stacked on top of each other. Lay out the two pieces of wood on top of the blocks. Make some benches with just one piece of wood and only one or two layers of blocks. Cover them with disposable plastic table covers pinned to the wood with thumbtacks. You can lay any outdoor decorations you choose on the tables. If you purchase the wood and blocks, it will cost approximately $220, but if you have connections with a contractor or anyone you can borrow from, it will cost you $0.

More Tips for the Consumer

As a consumer, you have every right to know about any company you hire to work at your event. You must ask all necessary questions in order to become comfortable with whomever you decide to hire. If you hire a caterer, bartender, banquet hall, or other contractors, you must ask some basic questions; since you are not in that line of business, you don't know everything that can go wrong unless you ask. Consider the following when selecting a caterer:

1. When you make appointments with caterers, the first few questions you must ask are whether they have a health-department permit, business license, liability insurance, and workman's compensation for their employees. For these items, you need to request written proof and ensure the documents are updated, current, and in effect.

2. Find out how many years the caterer has been in business.

3. Learn each caterer's location.

4. Ask if the caterer gives samples upon request from the menu choices.

5. Find out what the caterer provides in a package of food and presentation. Ask for a minimum of three to four menus as complete packages.

6. Ask to speak to the chef who will handle your food for the event.

7. Ask to see pictures of different events.

8. Ask how many people will be working your event.

9. Once the contract is signed, ask whether the caterer is going to adjust the price if the market cost for food goes up. Make sure the contract stipulates that the price cannot change once signed.

10. Meet with at least four or five different caterers before you make any determination as to who you will hire. When you do decide to hire a caterer, ask to see one of that caterer's events in action. Do not deal with any caterer who fabricates a story and refuses or ignores your request to observe a catering event.

11. Request samples from each caterer and at least four or five different references from the past six to twelve months. The references cannot be family members or friends of the caterer. They should be individuals from different areas.

12. Ask the caterers what their contracts look like. All contracts must be very detailed, with specifics of food, setup, and what they provide—for example, china, silver, glass, or plastic. Compare all contracts.

13. Be very careful. Many caterers don't present all of the small details, and you could end up paying a lot more money than expected. When you ask for a complete package, you must have everything

listed in the contract, because if you don't pay attention, some caterers will take advantage of you after you sign the agreement and exploit details that were omitted or not included. You want to have everything inclusive and tallied on one final bill.

14. Be sure you understand what you will be charged for waitstaff. This amount could end up being 20 percent of your entire bill.

15. One of the bigger tricks caterers like to use is giving you a nice price for low to average menus and then charging for a variety of rental items—which can be very costly and often more than the cost of the menu.

16. When you hire a caterer, make it clear that you do not want to be involved with or perform any of the management the caterer is supposed to do for you.

17. Start planning your catered wedding eight months ahead. If you wait until right before the event, you'll probably face higher prices or have difficulty finding someone qualified to cater your event.

18. If you decide to hire a bartender, make sure he or she has a good reputation and references. Be sure to ask prospective bartenders all the necessary questions, like how familiar they are with mixed drinks, liquor, beer, and wine; whether they have taken any bartending courses; where they received this training; and if they have any certificates to show you. These basic questions are necessary because when you hire a bartender for a one-time event, you really don't know much about him or her.

19. You must make sure the bartender wears appropriate clothes: black pants, white shirt, vest, bowtie, and black shoes.

20. When you decide to hire a caterer, you must ask what the waiters and waitresses will wear. Request black pants, black skirts, black shoes, white long-sleeved shirt, bow tie, and a black apron made for waitressing, not kitchen work clothes. The women working should not be permitted to have their hair down, and no tattoos can be showing on anyone for any occasion.

21. You must request a no-smoking policy for the catering staff when they are working in the service and reception area. Do not permit cell phone calls by staff at any time, or eating or drinking around the guests for the entire event. Also ask the caterer to ensure that the catering staff will not be loud.

22. Waiters and waitresses should be stationed throughout different areas within the reception space, so that in the event you need service, you don't have to search.

23. Once you have an agreement, provide a time when the catering staff can begin to pack up the catering equipment. Make it clear that the caterer is responsible for clearing the tables in the seating area of plates, cups, etc.

24. When you order your wedding cake, make sure it isn't delivered sooner than an hour before the event. Whoever delivers it must set up the table for the cake and not just drop it off.

25. If you want the caterer to cut the cake, you must have it in detailed your agreement, otherwise you will be charged extra.

26. Assign someone to coordinate between the caterer, disc jockey, photographer, bartender, and whoever else is involved. You will not have time to deal with any of these distractions during the reception.

27. Have a check prepared for all the people working for you during the event, unless indicated otherwise in the contract. Treat the caterers with respect. If you have a bad attitude communicating with the caterers, you can expect the same back.

28. When you hire a caterer, you cannot base your decision only on what friends tell you. Conduct your own research and determine if the caterer is qualified to handle your event.

29. The longer you wait to choose your caterer and banquet hall, the greater the chance you will face difficulties overall. Your chance to save money will become slimmer and slimmer.

30. To be sure of finding a qualified caterer with a good reputation requires, begin discussions approximately a year before your wedding day.

31. In general, only 10 percent of caterers are qualified to handle a large event successfully. You need to find someone who is well equipped and can provide full-sized catering so that you can get everything you need in an all-inclusive package.

32. When you determine who your caterer is, confirm that there aren't any middlemen involved with the end services. Choose one company that is able to handle everything so you'll have fewer headaches and hassles to deal with.

33. Many people think they are going to deal with several companies and get everything for a lot less, but this is incorrect. For example, if you have a budget of $10,000 for food, bar, decorations, table covers, and centerpieces, discuss this with your caterer. He or she will likely accommodate this budget and arrange all of it for the same price instead of having you run around to ten different places and still end up with the same cost. Save yourself the energy and many headaches.

34. When you decide to hire a qualified caterer, you must let him or her know exactly where the reception is going to be held. You cannot hire a caterer and subsequently share the policies of the banquet hall, or any other surprises.

35. When renting a banquet hall, determine which venue offers you the best value and options for the price. It can be very costly when you factor in all of the small details that are required.

36. Once you've decided which banquet hall to rent, confirm that it has full liability insurance, a health-department permit, and a city or county business license. Those are the first questions you want to ask, and documents you want to see with your own eyes. You have every right to request proof of these documents.

37. When you are lining up contractors for your event, have a notepad handy and be very organized. Write down all the questions you need to ask the contracting companies you plan to hire. If you come prepared with questions, you are not going to be taken advantage of. Don't work with any company that is unable or unwilling to answer your questions or is unclear about what it says or advertises. These contractors can cause you unnecessary problems if you continue to deal with them.

38. When you talk to any individual or company, conduct the conversation almost like an interview. This will allow you to see whether you want to continue dealing with these people. It is very important to get a good first impression.

39. When you prepare questions for catering companies, don't hesitate to ask about their credentials and don't hesitate to ask the toughest questions. This is how you will find out if you are comfortable with them. If they are not up to the challenge with prompt answers, then you have your answer.

40. Discuss your concerns with friends and family who can provide you with some ideas on potential issues that you can add to your query.

41. Do not shy away from bargaining or asking all questions that concern you. This is part of the way to remain within your budget and assure success.

42. Remember, when you set yourself a budget, it is imperative that you stick to it regardless. That is the only way to ensure you will remain within your budget.

43. Remember what your main focus is and how you want to allocate your money. Your guests will likely be most attentive to the food, presentation, and bar. These elements are the top aesthetic items that will appeal to your guests and be of primary importance in their enjoyment of the event. People will not pay as much attention to the disc jockey, the coordinator, how many flowers you have, or the decorations. These are not big factors in creating a memorable experience for your guests. If you want to watch your budget, pay close attention to the most important elements, as they can get expensive.

44. Florists are generally the most expensive element in any event. To save on cost, have one of your friends be the coordinator. You can get a quality disc jockey for a low cost as well.

45. Save money by ordering your own table covers on the Internet that will cost even less than renting them. You can get them in any color you want, and they can be bought by the dozen.

46. Make a strict rule for yourself not to borrow money for your wedding event. Many young people cannot get help from their parents because the parents can't afford it. My best suggestion to you is to have a small party and reception in your backyard or in your house for close family and friends.

47. Don't overestimate your finances and get into a financial hole for your event. Run tight but efficient.

48. Do not deceive yourself as to how much gift money you will receive from your guests. You shouldn't plan on what you will get, because it's unknown. Always pay with what you can afford from your own savings.

49. If you are dealing with a catering company that only offers cheap, low-quality menus, you can easily provide the same caliber of food on your own without paying a caterer.

50. Many of the caterers in the marketplace are not full-sized and all-inclusive. Many are ordinary restaurants, and some of them don't even have a health-department license. They are working in the shadows of legality, and if you pay a premium price, you should expect to receive the best you can. You do not want a caterer to provide you with a variety of stories and then try to brush you off. These deceptive caterers are good manipulators but are ultimately unqualified and will end up being very costly.

51. Of course, if you have plenty of money and resources to pay for your wedding, you are likely looking into high-quality caterers. There is no need to focus on or consider low-class caterers or small home-based operators.

52. Fully understand that when you hire a cheap caterer, he or she doesn't care much about presentation and quality, so expect very little of this. You get what you pay for. We call these one-time deal caterers.

53. Regardless of which caterer you hire, be sure to request that plastic wrap not be used on any hot foods. It is made from hydrocarbon and other organic compounds. It is not the healthiest product to use when you wrap up hot food.

54. For young couples getting married, the excitement may exceed their budget. Many people borrow money from the bank, credit cards, and any other possible sources to achieve their magical wedding. They even borrow from family members and friends, but they are forgetting one thing: somehow that money is supposed to be returned to the people it was borrowed from. They erroneously assume they are going to get enough money in gifts to pay it all back. I see many young couples who don't even have jobs and are struggling financially. If you don't want to owe any money but still want to have a fun and memorable event, you can get married with eighty guests for less than $1,000. See the menus at the end of this book.

Owners and Operators

Before you open your food business—or even if you are already in business—I have some suggestions and ideas for you. You must follow all the required rules and regulations and comply with any laws applicable to the type of food business you decide to operate. Many people in this industry approach the business they want to operate with a crude attitude and totally nonsensical thinking. I will give you a few tips on how to start the legal way and how to keep the books for your own safety and financial security.

If you want to start a food business and have never been employed in one, right from the start you're courting financial disaster because of your lack of understanding of what is really involved. You have to understand that caterers, restaurants, hotel kitchens, and bakery and pastry shops are uniquely different in operation and regulation, and of course there's no comparing fast food or hotdog stands. If you follow the rules from day one and make yourself an honest plan without unrealistic fantasies, you might have a chance for a good start. Before you open a business you must pay attention to the following rules:

1. Design your kitchen by creating a blueprint that lays out where all your equipment will be stationed.

2. Go to the health department with a layout of your kitchen. Discuss with the health-department official all the applicable rules and regulations.

3. Go to the zoning office (known as "code and compliance") and make sure you have the authorization in writing to ensure the location has been approved.

4. Go to the business office of the county or city you are in and fill out the appropriate forms for a business license. If you have any difficulties, ask the business office to help you complete the paperwork.

5. On your business-license application, you will see a question about how much income you expect to earn for the first year. Choose "less than $50,000." You can't reliably predict what your business will earn, so use the lower amount for the first-year prediction.

6. Contact several different insurance companies to price various products, including liability insurance, workers' compensation insurance, and coverage for your equipment. Elect the cheapest insurance premium offered for your business type. Check annually with different insurance carriers to see if you can get a better deal.

7. If you are opening a bakery or pastry shop, you aren't required to have a health-department permit. Rather, you will need to consult with and obtain approval from the agricultural department. However, the business license and insurance requirements remain the same as for any other business. The primary difference with bakery and pastry shops is that they don't use poultry or any other meat or seafood. With agricultural-department rules, you can work from your home or any room in it. If you work by yourself, you will not be required to have workmen's compensation insurance.

8. It is mandatory for every production kitchen to have a stainless steel three-compartment sink with an adjacent single hand-wash sink; stainless steel table; stainless steel oven and stove; and a hood system to cover the area above the oven and stove. It is preferable to have stainless steel refrigeration, a heavy-duty stainless steel cutting board, and stainless steel or aluminum pots. Do not use any wooden cutting boards or tables. You also need a variety of sharp knives, a desk for your paperwork, a file cabinet, and a hot-water heater. Use stage 5 lights in the kitchen so you can see that the food is clean and see what you are doing.

Under all sinks, there must be an open gap so you can actually see the water draining. You must have a grease trap. You must have a bathroom with a hand sink. You must have a disposable paper-towel hanger, small trash can, and sanitizing hand soap on both individual sinks.

On the floor, you must have rubber mats so you don't slide or fall. Your floor tiles must be ceramic or linoleum. The walls must be painted with high-gloss paint or something that won't come off when you clean them.

You must have a steel cabinet for all your chemicals and utilities. It is preferable to have ten-foot ceilings and four windows—two on each side—for air circulation. Ensure that you have enough power for your entire building. There must be a screen on any doors and windows. All clothes and jackets must be hung in the bathroom or office, if you have one.

9. To start a business, you must have enough capital to pay for equipment and operate the business. Never start a business using credit cards. It is absolutely out of the question. Never use your home as collateral to borrow money. Do not use your car as collateral. Do not borrow money against any stocks you may have in the bank. Do not allocate any of your future retirement savings as collateral. Do not be intimidated into borrowing money from an individual or entity with high interest, because it can get very ugly if things don't go well.

10. Discuss every single point with your spouse before you get involved with a business. Make sure there is no disagreement between you. One spouse should run the business while the other works elsewhere, to bring in a separate or independent income. This avoids dangerous personal conflicts. It doesn't matter who runs the business—you or your spouse. One of you need to brings a guaranteed income to the household.

11. Do not try to convince yourself that you can be a huge success. Thinking this way may put you in jeopardy, and everything you work for will crumble because you allowed some fantasy to enter your mind.

12. Learn and gain knowledge from the businesses around the area you work in—how well do they do and how long have they been in the business. Research statistics on how many business sales these businesses have per year.

13. Prepare yourself mentally and physically to do every possible job in or out of the kitchen so you don't have to hire more people for certain items you can do by yourself. You must work as many hours as needed with no excuses.

14. Take prudent precautions not to play too big. Play small but be effective so the money can stay in your possession and doesn't end up somewhere else.

15. Be prepared to deliver, cook, wash dishes, clean the kitchen, work weekends and holidays, and complete paperwork on a daily basis. This is the only way to save money, move forward, and succeed with a small business. Don't be one of those business owners who just wants to come and eat lunch and shake hands.

16. Never bring your problems from the business home, because it can create a fracture in your marriage and with your kids. Keep your family intact and in a healthy environment by not mixing family and business life.

17. Those who are starting a catering business or restaurant and are not interested in following rules from the beginning are jeopardizing their investment and their energy. A business cannot succeed if you don't follow all the rules and regulations. If you choose to not follow these guidelines, your business will not be successful.

18. Many people who start a catering business or restaurant do not have any related food-service experience. They haven't attended culinary school. They may have only worked as a dishwasher somewhere or helped with food prep in a kitchen. This is not good enough to open a business and expect to be successful. The reason so many of them fail and close every year is a lack of understanding and knowledge about the food industry, catering business, or restaurant business.

    Often, individuals who attempt to start a food business lack the requisite education, documentation, or certification. They start a business that is bound to be unsuccessful and fail. If you as a new owner are trying to open a catering business or restaurant, you must understand the consequences you will face because of your lack of understanding. You will start to feel the pinch right from the get-go, because those who open a business with no knowledge are not very calculated, are highly impatient, and expect everything to happen in the first month, hoping to get rich quick.

19. Those entering the catering business can be ranked somewhere between 1 and 5, where number 1 is the top end and 5 represents the bottom. Many of those with no knowledge or experience who get in the business end up falling into category 5, which is the worst. Those who have been in the business for a long time will not necessary fall into category 1 or 2 because they don't have the motivation, energy, or financing to push to the top, even with many years in the business.

    You don't have to do much to be on the bottom with a 4 or 5; it will come to you pretty quickly with a poor reputation. Being on top requires continuous success with various facets of your business. It starts with your public relations, experience, competence, the image of your staff (including uniforms), high quality equipment, and of course the quality of your food and presentation as well as consistency.

    To be on top, never use anything that is disposable. Have all applicable documents available and current. Be able to offer everything with no involvement of a third party. Have a clean delivery truck used only for the food operation. Have your own logo and signs that are uniform. Respond to clients immediately—and, of course, be civil at all times. Some individuals have a difficult time doing so. You will need a variety of well-published accomplishments to stay on top.

20. Before you open a business and settle on a location, do your homework and research the area's demographics. Determine the average income. If you are servicing a predominately blue-collar area where income is lower than more affluent areas, adjust your pricing structure and service to reflect realistic market values. Look at how many similar businesses in the area offer services similar to yours. When you start out, you will have existing competition and established businesses to compete against, so your fight is going to be greater right from the get-go.

21. Before you sign any real estate agreement, commit to only a short-term lease with the option of an extension. If you enter into a long-term agreement and the business doesn't do well, your only option will be to shut down and file bankruptcy.

22. Review all expenses on a monthly basis to see what you're going to need to spend just to keep the doors open. Include electricity, rent, water, sewage, and telephone bills. If you don't have the skill, hire an accountant to perform these duties.

23. Keep enough untouchable money to cover a minimum period of six months to support the business. This does not include your paycheck; more than likely, you won't be able to issue any paycheck to yourself in the first year. You must understand when you open a business in a new field, there is a three- to five-year tryout to become established. You must have this attitude in mind.

24. Know how you are going to survive with your personal bills that are unrelated to the business. Many who are starting a business don't have any financing available to support their personal bills. To keep the new business running and operating, they begin to borrow small sums of money they have invested in the business to support their personal expenses. This is how the end starts. They run to the bank begging for a small loan, reach for their Visa or MasterCard, or put their home, cars, or any other valued item into collateral to try to collect quick money to survive. That's a point you never want to reach, That's the beginning of the end.

25. Some individuals who enter the food business get a big idea to open a second and third location. They think if they have more locations they will have more money, but this is totally untrue. If you have one location, get the maximum productivity and efficiency out of that location. It is not about how many locations you have, but rather what you produce. My suggestion is that if you only have one location, put all possible energy into that one. Some people think they might open only for dinner, some only for lunch and dinner, and some for breakfast, lunch, and dinner. Only the last one uses the full capacity of the existing business. If you do not use it, you obviously didn't push it to the max. Instead of spreading to another location and doubling your headaches,

problems, and responsibilities, stay in one place because you are a small business. Do not conduct your small business as if you are a big corporation. Do not allow your fantasy exceed your reach.

26. Some owners fall into financial problems because the route they chose to take was the wrong one, plagued with a lot of miscalculation. They panic and continue into a decline because they are losing a lot of money on a daily basis. They are digging themselves into a bigger hole. The next step they look into is getting rid of the business as fast as they can. If this doesn't work as quickly as they want, they panic even more, so they reach a point where they just give it away to get rid of their debt and responsibilities. If they can't get rid of it, the next step will be bankruptcy. For many, this is the only solution available.

27. Protect yourself from day one and file to become either a corporation or a limited liability corporation. You're effectively protecting all of your personal assets.

28. If you get into the food business, you must have a lot of energy, both mentally and physically. You cannot slack off. You can only push harder and better to improve your business. There is always something new to learn to improve quality and make your business more efficient, and to build up your reputation and stay consistent.

29. Make yourself a rule to not steal any ideas. Create your own individual ideas and image to promote and enhance your business. People will notice and expect it. Try to be creative all the time.

30. If you start seeing your business decline, immediately investigate how to fix it with no delay. If your income from the business decreases, sit down and make all necessary cuts. Start with labor cuts and a decrease in your inventory. Do not buy with credit. Reorganize and regroup the entire business. The only thing you never ever cut is the quality of the food, presentation, and service. Customers don't have to know anything about your financial situation or the decline of your business. Keep it to yourself.

31. When you're in business, especially the food business, you will have many ups and downs with income and staff attrition. It will cause a lot of stress, but you must have a strong will. Don't let it get you down if you lose good employees or if it's the slow time of

the year as far as income. A variety of small problems may appear on a daily basis, and those can drag you into major problems. Overcome and deal with it.

32. Do not brush off any trivial problems or difficulties you are faced with. These types of things will slowly bring you into disaster and basically lead you to shut down your business.

33. As a business owner, you have to be humble. You can't have thoughts that you're second to God. You must quickly adjust your attitude. Your competitors might not think that way about themselves, and they will be willing to give much more effort and energy to work than you will.

34. You may sometimes lose electricity in your building, especially when you're located in a rural area where storms or strong winds can easily create a power outage. At a minimum, you need to be equipped with a large generator to continue operating the refrigerators in the kitchen and basic lighting, especially if you have little or no insurance coverage for food spoilage.

     If you happen to lose electricity in the middle of the night, by the time you arrive in the morning, many items may be spoiled and useless, causing a variety of problems. If there is a bad weather forecast, keep one person on standby through the night to immediately start the generator. If you wait too long, the rising temperatures can allow bacteria to start developing on the food.

35. If you're in the catering business, my suggestion is to have outdoor stoves, burners, and ovens that operate on gas in your storage building in case you have an event coming up and no electricity. Always have at least six canisters of gas on standby for emergencies. Place them outside behind the building and make yourself a fabric fence to protect dust and flying objects from entering your cooking area. You can then continue with your production for the event. You must also have at least five or six large coolers filled with ice so you can store cold items like meat and seafood. Have insulated thermo boxes as well for hot food storage. Always be prepared, because these situations happen when you least expect it.

36. Before every event you cater, when the food is already laid out on the buffet table, take photos of each item on the menu and one

of the entire buffet. File these with the contract and keep them together. You are now protected with photographic proof in case any questions arise after the event has concluded. Make sure the pictures you take have the date and time stamped on them. These photos can be used later in advertising for your company.

37. As an outside caterer, you will sometimes deal with people who come up with all kinds of fraudulent stories after the event. Any evidence you have—including contracts, pictures, and statements from crew members and witnesses—will help protect you. Sometimes these things happen even when you have done everything to the best of your knowledge. Even people who were happy at the event, shake your hand, and tell you how great you are can turn around a month or two later and post negative reviews on the Internet. Even minor allegations can be harmful, so protect yourself at all times from beginning to end.

38. When you're formalizing a contract as a caterer, make sure it contains very specific details for every aspect of the event. If the contract calls for a certain amount of people, count the tables in the seating area and the number of chairs at each table. It is very common for people to add more guests to the event after the contract has been signed. When they decide to add more people, they usually don't inform the caterer. This can cause higher labor and food costs, and many other inconveniences, if you're not aware of this situation.

39. As a caterer, agree on nothing verbally. That has the same durability as a signature written in ice. Remember, you are in the business to make money and to protect your business interest.

40. As a business owner of a restaurant, catering company, or any other food business, you should implement cardinal rules in the kitchen for you and your staff to adhere to. It is imperative that you have separate cutting boards for poultry, meat, seafood, vegetables, and fruit. Bread and pastries should have their own cutting board as well. These must be marked and coded with different colors to determine what they are used for. Often, the kitchen staff are unaware, unconcerned, and don't understand the importance of having several dedicated cutting boards. Many of these food

categories—like seafood and poultry for instance—carry a high risk of contamination from bacteria. If they're not washed thoroughly and you use them the next day for fruit preparation, you can make people sick.

41. As a precaution, all fresh products—such as seafood, meat, beef, vegetables, and fruit—must be soaked in cold water for several minutes and rinsed before you use them. Fresh food products are normally sourced from a processing center and placed into boxes by workers. This process of sorting and packing requires many workers to handle the items, and this facilitates transfer of disease and germs, creating a potentially serious health problem. You must stay on top of your kitchen staff at all times to ensure that they follow this protocol. Train your people so that anything coming out of your kitchen is as safe as possible.

42. As a business owner, you must carefully protect your assets from day one of your venture. If something happens to you and you're unable operate your business, what happens next? As a contingency, you should always have a designated second-in-command who can handle all necessary business decisions and legal documents. The lack of a person who functions in an executive capacity can create critical problems for the health your business.

43. From day one, your business protocols for paperwork, scheduling, uniforms, and the appropriate equipment must be consistent. If you start the right way, your business will not only run much more efficiently, it will also provide a model of understanding for everyone as to how you expect the business to run and operate. Definitely do not overlook these objectives.

44. You will want your catering business to be considered reputable and high-quality. One way to earn this honor is to make a crucial rule for yourself from the very start to not use prepackaged products of any kind. Never use canned food, avoid frozen food as much as you can, and produce meals on your own. People will know whether you used fresh ingredients or if you're one of those caterers who buys and preheats food.

45. Strive to have a creative menu for your catering business. Don't copy or replicate someone else's menu and presentation. This is a

very important point for your business, as word gets out quickly as to whether you're above average, average, or not good at all.

46. When creating a unique menu, work with ingredients that will be hard to duplicate easily. Many competitors will try to copy your menus. You want to be known as the only caterer in the entire region who people can point to and say you have high-end service and quality food. Create a strong image and maintain consistency with your business. That is the best way to gain a lot of business for yourself. Word of mouth is the best form of advertising.

47. Of course, the food must be good. Presentation must be excellent. Do not forget, whether you're dealing with an upscale client or someone more budget-minded, you must always treat your client with respect. Be polite and have a smile on your face. Negotiate in good faith and be articulate when you explain service details and contract terms. Frequently, clients will try to drive a hard bargain and push you to the wall to get more for less. While you cannot give in to these demands, at the same time, you must be polite and respectful.

48. In the catering and restaurant business, you must be prepared for clients to bargain with you and treat you as a low-caliber caterer during negotiations in order to extract higher quality for a lower price. Do not give in to these unreasonable demands; you are only hurting your profit and business. You do not want to take an operating loss when the cost of food and labor is high, so do not be discouraged or upset if you're unable to compromise with certain clientele on price.

49. In the catering business, if you're able to secure six out of ten events, you're in good shape. Don't try to grab everything that comes across your table, especially if the customer is not willing to pay a reasonable price to cover all of the expenses and profit for an event.

50. When creating a menu for clients, request a comprehensive set of details pertaining to the client's expectations for the entire package. Determine what the budget is and how much the client can afford to spend. You can then provide options with a range of price points. Calculate your expenses so that your average food expenditures will be limited to between 20 to 26 percent. For

more costly items on your menu, your food costs may need to go as high as 30 percent. Labor costs—including both kitchen help and waitstaff for the event—shouldn't exceed 18 percent.

This will leave you with approximately 50 to 55 percent profit out of the entire cost. If you allow your expenditures to exceed these figures, you jeopardize your profit margin. Think those numbers are not good enough for you? You're just fooling yourself. The main factor here is to purchase food appropriately and keep labor costs low for the event. This will allow you to be more profitable.

51. Be aware, when drafting a contract, that you must charge a 50 percent deposit upfront and ask that the remaining 50 percent be paid in full on the day of the event. The 50 percent deposit should not be spent on anything else; keep it in an escrow account and use it only when the time comes to purchase products for the particular event. Many business owners get excited over the payment and use the money for something else. Remember, your profit comes when the event is over, not before. That's the money you can and should plan on. You must be very smart about it so you don't jeopardize your funds beforehand.

52. Stipulate the start and end time of the catering event in the contract, so that you know when your portion of service ends. Based upon my experience, it is not uncommon for events to start much later than planned. Clients mistakenly believe the event begins when they arrive and forget what was agreed to in the contract. These situations can be costly to you as a caterer, as far as labor costs go for the waitstaff and cooks, not to mention the food that has been sitting longer outside, which can cause problems. When you draft an agreement, you must be very specific about all of the temporal details involved on the day of the catering.

53. When you cater at a banquet hall, church, synagogue, or any other venue, and you see that the kitchen is not clean or sanitary, it is your ethical duty to notify the health department immediately. If you or others ignore these problems, at some point it will become dangerous to prep food in an unsanitary kitchen. Don't ignore these health issues. Take charge and inform the appropriate authorities.

54. As a professional caterer, at some point you will do business with government agencies. Most of their disbursement requirements place a thirty- to ninety-day holding on funds before you are paid. You must understand these policies on payment, as many small businesses don't have the financial capability to wait such an extended period to be paid for their services. Before you commit to a catering job with the government, be sure you know what to expect in terms of a delayed payment process. If you don't have enough of an income stream to cover your expenses, these payment conditions can cause you serious financial problems.

55. If you plan to employ a part-time waitstaff for your catering business—who will only work on days you have an event scheduled—you must vet and verify information about each individual's background through former employment references. In addition, you must make it clear to each member of the waitstaff that earnings are based upon an hourly wage and any tips received. As the owner, you will need to keep written documentation of the hours each member of the waitstaff has worked. Pay the waitstaff an hourly wage for each event by check, and any tips received will come directly from the person hosting the party. You may also elect to set up a system with guaranteed tips so that the waitstaff feels more comfortable knowing how much money they will receive at the end of the night. You as an owner are not obligated to pay the tax on your employees' tips, or on wages if you limit each individual to a maximum of $600 a year in hourly salary. You must report anything above this figure and pay the appropriate taxes.

    Savvy catering-business owners rotate waitstaff to employ different individuals at different events rather than employ them on a consistent basis. That method allows you to keep each employee's yearly salary under $600. This is especially recommended for a small catering-business operator. This strategy is considered very controversial by some employees, however, and some owners are confused about it.

    As a business owner, it is not your responsibility to pay taxes on the tips the waitstaff collects. Waitstaff are required to maintain a record of their earnings (tips plus salary) and include tips with their total income when filing their own taxes. The owner will not have any knowledge of or ability to verify the amount received in tips. Therefore, it is not the owner's responsibility to carry the tax burden of an amount that waitressing might earn the individual.

56. Business owners for any food service with employees should have a camera installed in any area where employees work as a liability precaution. The same policy should apply if you are catering outside of your business facility at a private venue or different location. As a caterer performing services in another venue, you should inspect the venue to see if there are cameras already in the building and where.

It is not uncommon for unscrupulous employees to claim they were injured at work when there is no evidence to prove otherwise. This can create a hassle and inconvenience with unemployment, workers' compensation, and your insurance carrier. All across the country, these claims come up, and many of them are unfortunately false. However, accidents can happen from time to time, and these employees should be protected 100 percent. As an employer, you must provide workers' compensation insurance and any other option to protect your employees and yourself. This goes both ways.

57. Try to build up a strong image of your business by creating your own soups, dressings, and sauces. Avoid all canned goods and as much frozen food as you can. Do not keep a large inventory of fresh food products, as unused goods can quickly spoil. People will notice the difference between fresh and frozen or canned immediately. When it's all fresh, they respect your business more. This is one part of building your image properly, and you must be consistent with it.

58. When drafting the terms and conditions for a catering event contract, be wary of what I call the "extra 10 percent" often added after the contract has been finalized. While most of the guests in attendance will be adults, there will likely be a fair number of children who will attend an event as well. Occasionally, the host will attempt to avoid any discussion of meals tailored to children until the day of the event. Many hosts will try to persuade you to waive your fees for children's meals on the event day, reasoning

that children will not eat much. This practice will not only limit your profits but may well cause a shortage of food for the adults. This can have a noticeable impact on your service, especially when there are as many as twenty or thirty meals needed for the kids.

While you should gladly accommodate an additional kids' menu, you must charge full price for the meals. In reality, when kids go through the buffet line, they will take a regular meal on their plates. They then will not eat the entire serving they have taken, creating more uneaten waste than adults.

Incorporate a children's menu into your services and address this topic during contract negotiations. You should not budge on this subject, as it will compromise your profits and ability to serve the adult guests adequately. The client is always looking for a way to save money, and this is one area where you can expect to be blindsided if you're not prepared and aware of it during your negotiations.

If the client expects children to be in attendance, the contract should stipulate that kids' meals will be provided in addition to meals earmarked for adult guests. The kids' meals do not have to be as expensive, but the contract must be clear that these discounted meals are to be consumed by the allotted children and not uncounted adults. Often, clients will be deceptive on this point and attempt to save by having additional uncounted adult guests provided for with the less-expensive kids' meals. This is the reason to have separate menus for adults and kids. Never combine the two.

Be courteous and forthright when explaining this detail to clients. They must be presented with meal options for children, and these options must compensate you fairly. Explain what your limitations and terms are when catering an affair with children present. The important point to keep in mind is that you need to be reasonable when negotiating a contract and ensure that all details are included in it. There should be no changes to the contract after it is signed by both parties.

59. Many owners in the food business offer discounts like two for one, 50 percent off, or other price reductions in an effort to generate

business and boost profits. This strategy is highly paradoxical, and I consider it to be an early stage of failure before the business begins to fall apart. By employing such a concession, you will not only cheapen your service and reputation but also do irreparable damage to your business that can be difficult to reverse.

In the United States ever year, thousands of businesses come and go after a few years of service. When you start advertising "buy one, get one free" promotions, you become disadvantaged because you're providing your service for half the price just to stay in business. Your business exists to make money, not to lose it.

However, many financially distressed business owners will drag the situation out until they are flat-out broke and the business permanently goes under. Don't fool yourself into believing promotional tricks will keep you in business long-term. What you can do is reduce your prices a little bit on the menu. This will boost your business in a healthy way, allowing you to become more profitable and keep your reputation high with prospective clients.

60. When you perform catering outside of your kitchen—such as when an event is outdoors in a tent or field—you will need to have an elevated platform for your food supply and preparation station. The platform should be at least one foot above the ground so that all of your hot and cold boxes can sit on top of it. You cannot allow any of the catering equipment or food to be on the floor, as there is a good possibility that bugs will crawl into the boxes or work area and create a contamination risk. This can cause serious health problems. Avoid them by ensuring outdoor preparation is facilitated within a sterile environment.

61. All of your waitstaff and cooks must wear rubber gloves at all times. There should be a zero tolerance policy when it comes to handling any food with bare hands. Never handle, serve, or prepare food with bare hands. Guests will feel more comfortable knowing that the food they eat has been safeguarded as much as possible.

62. If you plan to perform outdoor grilling, always use real wood from the yard (or wherever you are able to procure some) and avoid the gas grill—it's unhealthy and the food won't taste as good. One advantage to grilling with wood is its ability to reach the best and most consistent temperature.

63. When you run a restaurant or any other food-preparation service, make it a habit to create and develop your own homemade dressings and soups, aiming for a point at which 99.9 percent of your food is consistently fresh. This is a prime way to build and keep a service reputation for quality.

64. Clients routinely come up with new and novel ideas to both save money and enhance their event, but they rarely talk about how much these last-minute changes end up costing, invariably laying the financial burden on you. This is the main reason to have a straightforward agreement in place that is fair and clear for both parties. There should be no gray areas open to interpretation.

65. Before the client signs the contract, you must both acknowledge that there will not be any changes in what has been agreed upon, especially when it concerns the payment expected for the services outlined. The only change that is reasonably acceptable would be an increase in the number of guest expected, as long as the change in guests brings a corresponding price increase. However, if the number of guests is reduced, you should maintain the original contractual terms without a reduction in your fees. The logic here is that you want to protect yourself should you be asked to cater a much larger same-day event that would have to be declined in anticipation of the current one.

    Never allow yourself to be manipulated into altering the agreed-upon contract from its original terms. You should also make sure deposits are nonrefundable. The deposit should consist of 50 percent of the entire cost paid up front, with the remaining half of the balance due on the day of the event. The final half of the payment must be in the form of a credit card, cash, or money order. Do not accept a check, as it can easily bounce. Collecting can then become very costly to you in attorney, court, and collection fees, not to mention the aggravation, inconvenience, and loss of your time. Stick to these payment policies to avoid these hassles.

66. As a business owner, general manager, or any other executive position in a restaurant, hotel, or privately owned business, avoid having a close relationship with your employees. Do not have a happy hour with them. This is the only way your employees will

respect you enough to speak out openly and honestly if something goes wrong. If you do have relationships with these individuals, you will likely have difficulties and conflicts in handling major business situations.

67. Before you hire any employee, request direct references from a previous supervisor. After you've spoken with the former supervisor to discuss the individual's performance, ask to talk to the person in charge of the entire business. Otherwise, you will never know if you received honest, direct, and truthful answers. It is always good to have the final word from the general manager or owner as to why the person left a previous position. This approach will lead to a better and more comfortable hiring decision.

68. Create a uniform policy for your cook, chef, waiters, and waitresses. Stipulate that all employees must have a second uniform available at all times so they can change if the uniform becomes dirty or begins to smell. Client and guests will not be pleased to see dirty servers or a cook or chef in dirty, sloppy, or ill-fitting attire.

69. Make sure there is no unnecessary equipment in the kitchen. Extraneous equipment accumulates dust, grease, rodents, roaches, and other insects. Often, kitchen staff will not give much attention to equipment that isn't in use. Make sure the kitchen area only contains equipment you will use regularly—nothing more and nothing less. You must keep the kitchen in an environmentally clean and sanitized condition while adequately complying with health-code requirements.

The Health Department

Can you imagine what food service would be like if we operated without a health department to oversee operations? Unfortunately, many catering businesses and mobile food operators conduct regular business without a health-department permit. Many small mom-and-pop businesses are operating without a valid health permit, and their home, garage, and minitruck lacks proper sanitary conditions. Those who operate without a health-department permit are operating a dangerous business.

Sadly, although health departments are well aware of these types of operations, they don't do enough to reprimand or shut such businesses down. What I've gathered from talking to field agents is that they lack manpower and are overloaded with work, so they are unable to adequately police outlying operators. Inspectors must go through a formal court procedure to shut someone down. In the area where I operate in a small county, there are at least three businesses operating without a license from the health department. On a couple of occasions, I have brought these to the attention of the health department, and no action has been taken.

After forty-seven years of experience dealing with health departments in various locales over the years, I suggest we stop going backward and begin the right way. You must obtain a health-department permit and business license. It is also mandatory to have some form of liability insurance. Finally, you must obtain approval from the zoning office in the area where you will conduct your business.

In my opinion, there is a dangerous lack of communication between the regulatory agencies that issue business licenses, health-department permits, and approvals from the zoning office. These three offices need to communicate more effectively and implement rules impervious to manipulation and loopholes. If there is no concerted effort to reform or fix these problems, we are going to have more and more illegal operations that can cheat on taxes easily and claim anything they feel like. These unlawful operations are detrimental not only to operators who follow the law but to consumers as well.

Such operations put unfair competitive pressure on legitimate businesses that follow all of the rules and regulations to assure lawful compliance while striving to maintain high standards of quality. While the owner in compliance works hard to meet legal obligations and tax burdens for the county, city, and state, those who lack the proper credentials and skirt the law have an easier time at the compliant owner's expense.

Each local regulatory agency points a finger at another agency, which in turn points a finger at the state. According to my local health department, the state has to pass laws for reform. This is the same response I received from the commissioner of revenue in my county. They suggested that I petition the state government to pass a law to correct the situation. It is perplexing when the health department itself is unable to address basic stuff they're regulating.

Many field agents in the health department have a conflict of interest, because they have fostered relationships that are too intimate and close with the business owners of restaurants and catering outfits. These relationships lead to an unhealthy inspection environment. When an agent has been inspecting the same business for a long time, he or she naturally becomes friendly with the owner. In my opinion, field agents need to rotate between different inspection jurisdictions every few months. They will get much better results on their inspections and also stay honest and preserve the integrity of their office.

In my experience as an executive chef working in hotels, I have found that many of the cooks and kitchen employees have a great disdain for the health department. They despise having to stay on top of things in the kitchen like cleaning, organizing, and other small factors the health department is required to look for. In order to really keep the kitchen environment healthy, safe, and sanitized, I would like to see the health department conduct inspections on a biweekly basis. By adhering to a more frequent schedule, inspectors will bring each food production and kitchen operation to a much safer and healthier level for catering and serving food.

It is important to recognize that one of the most important factors for food safety is the oversight and involvement of the health department. Business owners should seek to have the full support of the health department. In order to earn this support, we have to continuously prove to inspectors that we are on top of everything required and are complying with their regulations. The health department will back us up if something happens, and I can assure you we need that support if something inadvertent occurs.

As a kitchen operator, owner, chef, or cook, you have to treat the health department with respect, even if inspectors are pressing you with things you don't like or agree with. They are not there to harm you intentionally. They are there to help you. You might not even be aware of certain health discrepancies or have paid enough attention to them. Anything an inspector tells you to correct, correct promptly without resisting or bargaining. Many owners and staff try to walk away from these seemingly onerous regulatory requests and criticize the department. Remember, health-department field agents are just doing their job, so respect them by complying as necessary. It is in your own best interest.

The health department has, to my knowledge, very basic and limited requirements for a catering business, and almost no requirements whatsoever for outdoor caterers who cater outside of their premises. Most caterers that have to haul all of their food basically do whatever they want with no regulations. They can deliver food with any vehicle they choose, they can put food on the floor, and they can deliver without hot boxes or thermo boxes. They have no requirements to maintain proper, steady hot or cold food temperatures.

My conversation with some health-department officials has revealed that the health department does not have any printed guidelines as to how outdoor caterers should be equipped. They only have basic requirements for operating a regular kitchen, which has a completely different set of operating requirements distinct from the outdoor caterer. This brings home the point that many operators are unlicensed by the health department. The health department groups everyone under a health-department license, and this is not the way it should be. The requirements are totally different for different food operations.

The following are some ways the health department can crack down on illegal catering businesses:

- Anybody who is able to obtain a business license from the county or city must also get a health permit.
- Anybody who applies for a business license must furnish proof of a health-department permit.
- The health department needs to go on online to determine who advertises as a caterer in a particular area. Google, Yahoo, or any other available search engine can provide such information. It doesn't take long to find out who's operating illegally.
- The health department must institute a serious penalty for those operating illegally.

If the health department were serious about cracking down, no illegal operations would exist. It might seem a little extreme, but the rules must apply to all equally. The health department has the responsibility to ask every operating banquet hall to verify that every caterer operating on the premises provide an updated permit and inspection certificate.

What strikes me as unusual when I cater at a venue operated by either a museum or the local or state government is that these locations don't require that any health-department license or even a business license be presented. My conversations with the managers of these venues revealed an attitude that it is not their job to require a health-department permit or business license. This shows how far the health department needs to extend its reach. Why should so many businesses have to operate under health-department requirements when at least 10 to 15 percent of similar businesses are seemingly operating without any requirements?

Some banquet halls don't have a license to operate as a caterer. The only license they have is to rent the building facilities out, not to operate as a full-size caterer or do anything associated with the preparation or serving of food. These operations should be penalized when in violation, otherwise they will continue without any health-department oversight. If the health department were stronger and more independent, most of these unregulated businesses would cease to exist. The penalties must be consistent, severe, and intolerable.

Anyone who opens a food business or operates a kitchen serving others should have a basic culinary-school education or training and not just a quick course through the Internet. If a hairstylist in most states has to have between 1,500 and 3,000 hours of experience, and an electrician or plumber is required to have education and training requirements to practice, then why are individuals who are preparing and serving food not required to have any objective expertise or formal training? No one knows better than health-department officials what kind of outcomes can occur and what food-borne diseases come from improper food handling that happens when uninformed persons are cooking and serving the consumer. This is a huge shortcoming of the health department. Although this is a major issue, it is easier to just not have any requirements and let people do what they like.

The health department only wakes up and takes action when a major health problem erupts or some dangerous transferable disease gets into food. When the authorities do wake up and address the issue, they raise a lots of questions as to what happened. It seems to me that the top people in the health department are aware of how poorly some catering businesses and restaurants are run. If the health department were more diligent in its inspections and enforced its policies, it would eliminate unscrupulous operators, leaving more qualified and caring operators involved in the cooking industry. This would safeguard consumers from illness and provide a healthier environment.

To my knowledge, there aren't any substantial health safety guidelines for a regular kitchen regarding use of glassware for cooking and mixing and the need for separate cutting boards for seafood, poultry, meat, and vegetables—or if you are allowed to use a wooden cutting board or a plastic one. It is unacceptable when you don't have basic guidelines as to what you can and can't use.

The health department has the power and influence to correct any unregulated areas that are contributing to lowered standards in the food-service industry. To improve conditions and eradicate these problems, stricter requirements and standards must be created in partnership with the surgeon general of each state. The local county surgeon general must be consulted and work alongside the health department to implement necessary safeguards. Ultimately, the health department must be more stringent in the creation and enforcement of health regulations. This is the only way to achieve a higher level of safety in restaurants, caterers, and other food services.

The general public has an unshakeable trust in health-department oversight. They have an enormous amount of confidence in the health department's ability to effectively police rogue operators in the food-service industry. Unfortunately, much of their trust and confidence is naïve and unfounded, and they are generally unaware of the lax attitudes and regulations that exist.

The health department should theoretically have a strong interest in maintaining a perception of high standards when it comes to consumer food safety. Such a reputation should be backed by stronger rules and regulations that are enforced in practice. If a few hundred people become sick and end up in the hospital because of lenient health regulations, they are going to begin asking tough questions of operators. Unfortunately, because the current rules and regulations in existence are quite lax, the blame will lie with the health department. The lack of proper regulations and enforcement is something the consumer isn't fully aware of.

The health department needs to increase health standards by implementing more effective regulation and compliance for all food services. In particular, the current rules for outdoor caterers must be augmented to much higher standards because of the increased risk involved with preparing and serving food outdoors, especially in hot and humid temperatures.

As much as caterer desire to be protected by the health department for affirmative compliance, the health department must protect itself from difficult questions if something dangerous happens because of poorly guided regulations. When widespread food-borne illness does occur, the narrow and limited regulatory requirements currently on the books will be heavily scrutinized and determined to be unsatisfactory.

When discussing health-department regulations, specifically those that apply to caterers, it becomes evident that the health department is out of touch. This is mainly due to the fact that the basic regulations are painted with too broad a brush and cover too many varied operations under one umbrella. A one-size-fits-all approach prevents any appreciation for the nuanced distinctions between different types of food-service operators.

My observation of health department officials—from field agents all the way to officials at the top—is that they lack any formal education or experience in any facet of the food-service industry. The majority of them lack hands-on culinary experience and have never been directly involved with kitchen operations, restaurants, or catering. The conduct and methods employed by these inspectors reveal very basic requirements for compliance that don't go far enough in protecting consumers from poorly run operations. These basic requirements are applied too broadly and are clearly insufficient for some food sectors. They fall woefully short of safety for the type of operation being policed.

In order to create appropriately stringent rules for the various types of consumer food services, an inspector needs to have experience with all the details related to the specific business or operation. The lack of differentiation for safety rules between caterers and restaurants indicates a level of dysfunction within the health department.

Over my years in the kitchen, I have seen almost everything imaginable. The truth is, most of the health-department agencies and their personnel have either two- or four-year college degrees—which is commendable, but not adequate for the health concerns I've addressed. You can't acquire the necessary skills, judgment, and experience required for this field by sitting behind a desk in a classroom. This has been proven time and time again.

It is extremely important that every kitchen have a minimum of two refrigeration units. This is to isolate the two types of storage required for safety reasons. One unit should be dedicated to storing food products that are delivered or received, and the second unit should contain only prepared food for storage. You risk serious contamination when you mingle two different groups of food. You cannot store prepared food in the same compartment with dirty boxes of produce and raw seafood, meat, poultry, or any other uncooked food that is delivered. These boxes come off a truck where they have been exposed to foreign bacteria, dirt, sand, and other unsanitary debris found on the floors of shipping facilities and delivery trucks.

It may seem extreme, but food-service kitchens usually have at least two or three separate refrigerators. It is very feasible. If you happen to have a large walk-in refrigerator, you can divide the room in two, with prepared food stored on one side and bulk delivery on the other.

All received food products must be removed from delivery packaging and marked with the date received. Never mix recent deliveries with older deliveries. Everything must be labeled and stored in clear plastic containers. This should be a basic requirement of the health department for all kitchens to comply with.

Most food-business owners dislike having the health or agricultural department around, breathing down their necks. They tend to be uncomfortable because they often fail to meet even the basic requirements for food safety. Even though the basic health requirements for some operators are quite lenient, they are still unable to adequately and consistently comply. Yet the basic requirements must be increased so everyone is held to a higher standard.

It is imperative that regulations for outdoor caterers in particular be vastly improved to ensure a safer environment for consumers. One day at a wedding reception, I observed an outdoor caterer station a cooking grill immediately adjacent to a public restroom. The grill was no more than seven or eight feet from the entrance. As the guests were coming and going from the bathrooms, you could easily detect the odors from within pervading the entire cooking and preparation area that was set up, risking possible food contamination.

What was surprising was that this event was catered by a very large company. It was shocking to see how few precautions were taken in serving almost two hundred people. The food was transported and stored on the floor of a rented delivery truck, with none of the food separated or stored properly in thermal or cold boxes. None of the basic equipment requirements for an outside caterer were followed. Even worse, the cooks were smoking over the grill.

Where are the specific, individual regulations that should be tailored to different operations unique to banquet halls, caterers, and restaurants? Restaurants are not caterers and vice versa. Equipment requirements must be different and applicable to the specific type of operation involved. There should be differentiation between the licensing requirements of caterers an restaurants. They cannot be under the same type of license.

From my experience, I recommend that when you are using fresh fruits and vegetables, soak them in a bucket of very cold (not freezing) ice water for ten to twenty minutes. This process will sterilize them more effectively than washing them under a faucet of running water. You must only perform this process shortly before you intend to use or serve them. This will preserve their flavor and consistency while ensuring they are clean from contamination.

Management and kitchen personnel generally prefer to ignore health-department rules and regulations. These individuals see the rules and regulations as annoying and interfering with their regular work schedule or routine, so they are more apt to hide or manipulate anything perceived as noncompliant. Much of the kitchen staff will do this to the greatest extent possible, as they are not in favor of too many burdensome regulations. In many cases, they are not following the requirements as expected.

As disturbing as it may sound, many kitchens have serious infestations of rodents, bugs, and roaches, along with dirty refrigeration units, unsanitized stoves, hood systems dripping with grease, and many other alarming issues serious enough to shut them down. Unfortunately, many of these businesses are still operating because they just get a slap on the wrist from the health department along with an idle warning. Such ineffective penalties are not good enough and allow unsafe kitchens to continue operating, to the detriment of the public.

Many restaurant and catering kitchens do not maintain proper temperature conditions for fruit, vegetables, meat, and seafood, which need to be kept on ice when they are worked on à la carte. You cannot take fresh products from storage and leave them on the table without any ice protection. Anything that comes out of refrigeration that will not be used within the next five to ten minutes must be set directly on ice. This rule is necessary because the ambient temperature in the kitchen is invariably warm if not hot most of the time. These warm temperatures are conducive to rapid food spoilage, and precautions must be adhered to so as to prevent any unwanted and dangerous putridness. Being on top of details like this is often seen as a nuisance, so kitchen staff often neglects to maintain the proper conditions.

As many of you are aware, excessive grease on top of the stove and inside the hood ventilation system is not just a hazard to sanitation safety but also a tremendous fire hazard. The health department, without excuse, must be more assertive and persistent in ensuring operating kitchens are free of this serious and overlooked danger.

Most untrained people can immediately tell whether a kitchen is clean and safe. If you walk through the kitchen, pay close attention to the condition of the floors and the underside of tables. If you see any evidence of food or food peels, you can assume the rest of your inspection will not be favorable. If you find problems with keeping a floor clean, you will definitely find much greater issues the deeper you probe.

I determined many years ago that the reason it's so difficult for business owners to keep up with the regulations of the agricultural and health department is the higher labor costs and supplies required, not to mention the energy and attention it takes to stay on top of preventive measures. In order for us to maximize safety, we must go above and beyond when complying with all pertinent regulations.

In many instances, the health department will inform business managers when they can expect an inspector to visit to their premises. On the one hand, it graciously allows the owner an opportunity to clean up the kitchen before the inspector arrives; on the other hand, it is obviously unethical and fosters an artificial level of compliance. In order for an inspection to be truly effective, it should be unannounced and conducted during an operation's busiest time to see whether the outfit is honestly in compliance. Even though it may be an inconvenience for the business to be inspected during a high-volume time, it is a realistic window into whether the operation is in full compliance.

When inspectors from the health department are conducting kitchen inspections, they should be required to have some type of surveillance camera affixed to themselves so that the inspection being conducted is documented and recorded. This protocol for documentation would ensure fairness and objectivity should there be a registered violation that might be in dispute. I realize this may sound extreme, but the intention is not to get someone in trouble; rather it is to maintain objectivity in addressing and correcting potential violations. Such a system would preclude any corruption or verification should a dispute arise.

The health department must implement and codify rules specific to the equipment used during kitchen operations—rules like prohibiting glass equipment; old and unused equipment; and any utensils with rust forming on them. Further, any utensils used in the kitchen like knives, mixing utensils, and so forth, should be separated and kept in clear plastic containers.

The health department must also have clear and precise rules for kitchen sinks. A kitchen must have a separate sink or a large mixing bowl designated exclusively for washing fruits and vegetables. Fruits and vegetables must be soaked in cold water for a minimum of ten to twenty minutes prior to usage.

Additionally, the health department's purview must extend into the kitchen's cleaning environment. There must be strict rules governing the methods, products, and procedures required in maintaining the cleanliness of the kitchen area. If the health department were more strict and straightforward in policing the cleanliness of the kitchen, I believe the ball game will change.

Insurance Companies and Business Insurance

As participants in the business community, we cannot operate our businesses without the various kinds of insurance required. Some common types of insurance you will need are commercial, liability, building, equipment, workers' compensation, vehicle, and any extra insurance necessary for financial protection. It is no secret that insurance companies love us because they make an enormous amount of money off food-service operations.

As business-minded individuals, before we commit to any insurance carrier's policy, we should do extensive research on a range of different companies. We need to determine who is the best fit for us as far as coverage and affordable premiums go. When possible, try to package your collective liabilities under one company. It will usually be more cost-effective to do so; however, if this is not the case, you must be prepared to split your coverage among several insurance carriers. As an example, you might be able to obtain a commercial package with one company while you get a better deal with another company insuring you for both workers' compensation and your trucks. If you're unaware of this and don't bother to split your insurance policies, it can end up costing you a few thousand dollars extra each year. So be careful in choosing.

In my thirty years as a business owner, I have switched insurance companies about six times. You will find that you can save a fair amount of money by doing this, which can then be reinvested back into your business. Two or three months before your annual insurance policy expires, start researching other carriers to see whether you might find a better deal. I would also suggest negotiating with your current carrier to see if a rate reduction is possible as well.

Before you sign with any insurance company, you must carefully examine the terms and read between the lines. Otherwise, you may find that something you overlooked will go against you. Have a lawyer proofread it. This will be well worth the cost.

Insurance companies are eager to gain your business, but there is a downside to you that can benefit them should a claim arise. The following are questions related to the catering business that insurance companies neglect to ask when drafting your policy:

- Where do you work?
- What locale are you operating in?
- Do you possess a health-department permit?
- Do you possess a business license?
- Have you been in the business previously?
- Have you filed bankruptcy in the last five years?
- Have you conducted a background check on your employees?

- Are you approved by the zoning department?
- Do you have fire department approval?
- Are you hauling your food to another location?

It is only after a claim is made that they begin to ask important and pertinent questions regarding your core business operations. These untimely questions can have a negative impact on the outcome of your claim and portion of liability, so it is important that you be aware of these potential problems.

The only interest insurance companies have in your business is how much money they can get by providing basic insurance. If something unfortunate happens like food spoilage, a building fire, or any other legitimately covered insurance claim, they are theoretically supposed to cover these claims. The interesting thing is that they will work diligently to take apart your claim and decline coverage if possible. Questions they hadn't bothered to ask when drafting the policy are now being asked. They are going to raise every question imaginable to try to pin you down and hold you responsible for as much as they can.

The answers to the questions I mentioned before will work against you if you haven't played by the rules and registered as dictated by lawful requirements. If you aren't in compliance with these licensing requirements, the insurance company will work hard to find any loophole in your policy to avoid paying out rightful claims. You must be very careful when applying for coverage by laying out exactly how your business operates. Do not hide information, and do not ignore relevant facts. Make sure these details are in writing on your policy and not verbally agreed upon, as this is meaningless.

Prior to any renewal of your insurance policy, you will receive an audit of your business. The sole purpose of this auditing request is to extract more money out of your business in the form of higher premiums. When you look at the big picture, your equipment and the structure of your business are getting older and, thusly, depreciating in value. Do not budge with the insurance company. It exists solely to get as much as it can from you, so pay attention and don't fall into the trap. An insurer's mode of operation is to charge you more while trying to reduce your coverage as much as possible. Take these precautions when it is time to sign the papers, as it will be very costly to if you fail to pay attention to their rapacious tactics.

When an insurance company performs an audit on you, it wants to know exactly how much money you are making on gross sales. The company wants to basically be your partner without putting any effort or investment into your business. Do not go along with this. Search a little more to find more favorable terms and conditions.

Keep in mind, when you are searching for an insurance company through your agency, that you are dealing with a broker who works on behalf of many other carriers as well. You need to be very specific with agents about what they intend to provide you, because they receive their commission from the company they arrange the policy with. You must be persistent with your agent to get the best deal.

When you are securing a commercial insurance policy in the food business, it is incredibly important to have a policy that adequately covers food spoilage and damage in case of a power outage. Failure to have a solid, airtight policy covering such events will cost you many thousands of dollars worth of damages. You must unequivocally put more attention, effort, and money into covering this potential calamity and worry less about preemptively repairing your old equipment. Put your money into the policy that has been providing coverage so that you have immediate assistance when the claim needs to be covered.

If you own your building, be honest with yourself and ask what it will realistically take to restore the building to its former condition. The insurance company is going to try to steer you toward the broadest, most expensive coverage it can sell; try to avoid this unnecessary cost. Studies show that the overwhelming majority of business owners diligently protect their property and are not interested in intentionally damaging their property to file a false claim. So try to cover the restoration out of your own pocket, and don't inflate the value of your business, because you will likely not need the insurance coverage—unless you're an unethical person with every intention of collecting money from your insurance.

When you're ready to sign an insurance policy, proceed very conservatively in itemizing your income and assets. Avoid using high estimations for your income, equipment, facilities, vehicles, or anything else. Be reasonable. Start off with a low monthly payment structure, and if you need to increase coverage on your policy, you can easily accomplish this with a quick phone call. Insurance companies dislike it when you decrease your coverage, and they will make it difficult to do so. It is prudent to start slow and low and leave your options open. You can save several thousands of dollars annually by adhering to this practice. It is the best way to go.

Remember that as a business owner, you are always in control. If you aren't satisfied with the terms and conditions your insurance company is providing, or if the company has negatively changed your policy coverage, you can easily get rid of it. However, before you cancel your existing insurance, make sure your new policy is in effect. You don't want to have a lapse in your insurance coverage, ever.

Before you commit to and finalize an insurance policy, you must be honest, truthful, and realistic about every facet of your business and its operations. It is a good practice to submit copies of all your licenses so that if something were to hypothetically occur in the future, you have covered yourself legally. Even if certain documents are not required, submitting as much business-related documentation as possible will ensure your policy is legally defensible. Retain copies of anything you've submitted and keep it filed along with your insurance policy.

Decorations

Take a round log approximately eight by sixteen inches and wrap long strips of fresh ivy around it. Start from the bottom of the log, and go all the way up so that the bottom is wider and tapers as it gets to the top. You can use this as a centerpiece or for the buffet table display. During Christmastime, wrap Christmas lights around the log between the ivy. You can also add little pieces of cotton between the ivy as snow.

Use long strips of ivy to decorate the center of a table. You can also use it in the buffet line by hanging the ivy on the skirting and on the actual table.

Aluminum buckets are really cheap. Try to get some with a height of eight inches and fill them up to the top with pine needles. Choose what colors you want the buckets to be and paint them a couple weeks prior so that the paint doesn't smell and you can wrap a ribbon around the middle. Bucket can also be filled with any other fruit or vegetables you choose, such as lemons and limes. Bundles of red grapes would look nice. The buckets can be used for a centerpiece for each table in the buffet line.

Catering Under $1,000 for Eighty to One Hundred People

Remember this if you want to save a fair amount of money on an important event: if you hire a company, it will cost you several thousand dollars; if you handle it on your own with my instructions, it will be under $1,000 for the whole event. Many people don't realize that it is possible to work with a low budget and still have a beautiful event. It all depends on you and whether you choose to go that route.

Of course, if you have the money, this is not for you. This subject of saving money comes as an idea from many years of experience with young couples and families who don't have the money but still want to do something nice. You have to be aggressive and really want the right event for a low budget. There are many tricks here for you to look at, from purchasing products to cooking to your setup to decorations and finally to your impressive event. You will find out how much money you can save by being serious about doing the event on your own.

In my experience in the catering business, many young people borrow money—if not from the bank, through Visa and MasterCard. They run to family members or friends, and they are just digging themselves a hole right from the beginning with all the money that they borrow. Go with my suggestions instead of taking on so many commitments and having to pay people back. You'll save all those thousands of dollars.

Your guests don't care where you do your wedding or party. They will give you presents either way. They will respect you because you did the wedding instead of paying the big operator. So you save money by doing your own work and you collect money from the presents. You are gaining from the whole situation if you go my route.

I will present you with several different complete menus that have good and fresh food, well presented, that you and your guests will be proud of. I will guide you point by point to do your own event. The following is some of the equipment and supplies you're going to need:

- home-style stove and oven
- two refrigerators
- cutting boards
- a few knives
- water sink available
- trash can

- plastic wrap and foil
- a few large pots and pans
- working area—table or counter in the kitchen
- hand mixer
- flour, eggs, milk, margarine, salt, pepper, garlic, spices, and other basics

Most homes have these available except for an extra refrigerator and a few large pans. Go to the trade post and buy yourself a spare refrigerator; they average $50 a piece, and there are plenty of them on the market. Clean it up, put it in your garage, and make sure it runs well. The pots can be cheap aluminum, and a hand mixer should cost around $10. In total, the items you don't have should not cost more than $200, and you may even be able to borrow these items for a few days. You must have these items three to four weeks prior to your event; keep them in your garage.

Next, you must quickly plan your decorations, all from around your home and outside. Go to my decoration page on how to save money on decorations. Pick up whatever you feel is going to be easy for you. Prepare all your decorations, if possible, ten days before your event. You must choose without any confusion what you want your event to look like. Remember, the idea is to save money and not to spend it.

If you do the event outdoors next to your house in the country or the beach, you have to plan everything according to the location. Remember, outdoor events can be very tricky as far as the weather and Mother Nature go. If you have a double garage, you could probably accommodate your guests there if the weather is bad. So just in case, you must clean up your garage. Take everything out of the garage and put it behind your house, covered with a tarp. Paint the garage at least ten days prior to the event. Put some appropriate lights there and make it comfortable. By doing this, you save the $1,500 to $2,000 it would have cost to rent a room.

One thing you don't want is all of the guests using the bathroom inside your home. Contact a few companies about getting a Porta-Potty. Get two of them: one for women and one for men. So far, this is the biggest expense you have.

An event with no music is dead. You must create an atmosphere by using the music you choose. If you have four speakers, place them in each corner of the area, and don't have the music loud. You save thousands by not using a disc jockey or a band. If you don't have speakers, borrow them.

You can make your reception or party attractive even if guests aren't going to wear suits. Note on your invitation to come dressed casually and comfortably. You have to remember, your reception is all about having good food and presentation. You're probably going to need some of your friends and family to help out.

If you decide to do your catering event for under $1,000 for eighty to one hundred people at home in your backyard—or any other place convenient to you with no rental expenses—you will be able to purchase beer and wine but not hard liquor. It all depends on which kind of menu you will choose; some of the menus are under $500 and some are over. This could make a big difference on your budget. If you use the menu under $500, you will have the option to purchase beer and wine and still remain under your budget.

If you do provide beer and wine, you must have an ABC license. The number of people you're inviting makes it a full-size catering event and not a small private party. You want to protect yourself by complying with all legal licensing. Remember, when you have a bar with alcohol, you must separate your bar from all of the soft drinks. The reason is if you have underage guests, they should not have any access to or an excuse to be around the bar.

You must apply for the ABC license at least one month prior to your event. You can apply on the Internet. For beer and wine, the license will cost you approximately $55 to $65 for one day. For hard liquor, it will probably cost you $10 to $20 extra. After you apply and pay with your credit card, you will receive a confirmation through your e-mail.

Make sure you have your license posted on your bar; you might get a surprise visit from an ABC agent, and if you don't have a license, you will be penalized. You will need to appear in court, and it can cause a variety of inconveniences and unnecessary fines.

The arrangement of the buffet tables will depend on where you've chosen to do your serving. Consider the following:

- If you decide to do catering in your garage, separate the buffet into two different sections against the wall. Put the hot food on one side and the cold food on the other. For decorations, tie granaries, pine leaves, bamboo, and big branches eight to ten feet high to the walls with greenery. Skirt and cover your buffet table and drink station. Green and white work well all year long.

- If you do your event in a tent, put the buffet in the center. You will need two rectangular six-foot tables and one round sixty-inch table. Put the round table between the two six-foot tables in the center. Make sure they are all put together. Put skirts on them, and you can level up the tables with little pieces of cardboard. Cover them with tablecloths and top with your display food. You must leave enough space for a few chafing dishes and the hot food.

- If you cater inside the house, you must spread the food out in a few different areas. You do not want everyone to accumulate in one area. Use the kitchen, dining room, and living room.

- If you cater under a pergola, you can place your buffet tables along the longer side of the pergola.

- If you decide to grill at your event, use six-foot tables and put the grill in the middle between them. Put your chafing dishes on one side of the table, and have one table for all your cold items.

It doesn't matter where in the house or backyard you're going to do your wedding reception: you have to remember that when you choose to go with a $1,000 reception, you have to stick to it. If you get sidetracked, you will go over budget, and you aren't serving the purpose of saving money.

All the menus in this book will be within your budget. You can use your own knowledge and imagination to create your own menu, but keep it under $500. If you exceed that, you start facing a problem with your budget. The menus I suggest run right on target with the price and the convenience of doing it yourself. When you choose a menu, purchase exactly what the menu calls for and stick to it; you might have money left for beer and wine.

To stay on-budget, you must consult the decorations suggestion list I provide, because 98 percent of the decorations I list do not have to be purchased. You must understand that you can't increase the number of people, because your budget will not allow it. If you decide to increase the number of guests, it will cost you more money.

You will need to have friends and family help you put everything together. Organize and allocate tasks. It is not complicated to perform your own catering, but you will need assistance. You must lay out everything on paper and then sit down with friends and family and put your package together. That is the only way you will succeed in creating a successful event.

If you cater your own wedding, you will probably be under a little bit of stress because of your desire to make your wedding memorable. The less you pressure yourself, the better off you will be. Any other event or reception you do, you will be much more comfortable with it. Remember, if you can add $200 to $300 to your budget, you will have much broader options to choose from.

When you invite guests to your reception, the guests will likely want to have good food and drinks available in a comfortable atmosphere. Something to consider when you do your own event is to make sure the entire environment surrounding the reception is comfortable for the guests. I suggest light music until everyone has eaten, and then you can switch to whatever you want.

Hold your ceremony in the same location as your reception. You will save a lot of money by doing it this way, and most of the guests, from my experience, like the idea of having everything in the same place.

You can purchase many of the items you will need several weeks ahead or longer. You may be able to resell them after the event for full price or at least 75 percent of what you spent on them. In addition to the items mentioned earlier, the following are items you will definitely need for your cooking, display, storage, and presentation:

- six disposable table covers—$6
- three disposable skirts for the buffet table—$10
- decorations, free from nature—$0
- four chafing dishes, the lower-grade type made for picnics—$18
- approximately ten disposable serving trays for cold food—$15
- approximately ten plastic mixing bowls for food preparation—$15
- fifteen full-size aluminum pans for cooking and roasting and for the final hot food display—$9
- half-size aluminum pans—$6
- ten individual Sterno cans for the chafing dishes—$10
- 200 white China plates for serving—$13
- 120-piece combo pack of clear disposable forks, knives, and spoons—$12

- 200 nine-ounce clear plastic cups for cold drinks—$8
- three or four large pots, between sixteen and twenty-four quarts for cooking, borrowed if possible from a church, school, or other organization—$0
- two large coolers, borrowed if possible from friends—$0
- at least four or five small bags of ice—$10 to $12
- sixty-cup coffee percolator, rented—$12
- eight pitchers, either glass—$40—or plastic—$16

With the items mentioned here plus the ones mentioned earlier, your total will be between $330 and $350. You still have approximately $150 left in your budget. That money could probably cover your beer, wine, and cups. If you decide to make a temporary pergola, then you will need to put $80 to $100 of that money into framing it.

You can make your own wedding cake for eighty to one hundred people for twenty or thirty dollars. I will explain in the menu the portions and how to do it. You can have three layers with three different flavors—for example, chocolate, vanilla, and red velvet. Make your own quick and easy icing, and add any filling you want to. It's important to serve a wedding cake and not cupcakes or any other combination. A wedding cake is a symbol of the wedding. It is a once-in-a-lifetime affair. Cupcakes are not for a wedding.

The cake will be made of stacked layers twelve, ten, and eight inches in diameter. You will need a three-foot white ruffle, and you will need fourteen-inch round of cardboard wrapped up with foil. You will also need a ten-inch round of cardboard not wrapped up with foil and an eight-inch round not wrapped up either.

The icing will be made from scratch. As for the cake mix, you can do it from scratch on your own, but of course it will be easier to use a cake mix. For the size of the cake I mentioned, you will need three chocolate cake mixes for the bottom layer. For the middle layer, you will need two vanilla mixes, and for the top one, you will need one cake mix in whatever flavor you want. You can bake the cake three to four weeks ahead, as long as you freeze and wrap it well. When you bake your own wedding cake, make sure it's partially frozen. This way you can fill it up with your choice of homemade icing. As a filling, you can use raspberry jam, strawberry jam, chocolate filling, or any other flavor you choose.

For the cake mixes, you will need a total of eighteen eggs. For the icing, you will need two pounds of vegetable shortening, four pounds of powdered sugar, eight ounces of margarine, one tablespoon of vanilla extract, and a touch of salt. In a mixing bowl, beat the shortening for four to five minutes with a hand mixer. Reduce to a low speed and start adding powdered sugar. When the powdered sugar is mixed in, increase the speed and add the margarine and vanilla. Keep beating it until the icing becomes fluffy. If you want part of the icing to be chocolate, you can add a few tablespoons of dark cocoa powder or some chocolate frosting. Mix it well, and you have chocolate mocha icing. The icing can sit out; it does not have to be refrigerated unless you're using it in a hot season.

When you are doing your own catering and working with a budget of approximately $500 for food, make sure you're not exceeding that budget. The menus I am going to present to you are not extreme and fancy, but they are well presented, they taste good, and they are all fresh.

In most cases, when you hire a caterer, you will not get the freshest products, and certainly not with a $500 budget. For each menu, I will give you the quantity you need, which is going to be for eighty to one hundred people. You have to make sure, when you purchase your items, to take with you a note pad and pen. Every time you pick up something for the menu, write the cost down. Otherwise, there is a good chance you will end up paying more than what your budget allows. Definitely do not use canned products. If you cannot use a certain fresh item because the cost is higher, you can use frozen, but it is not preferred.

Several items on each menu can be prepared weeks prior to the event and frozen. For example, some meat, poultry, seafood, and vegetables can all be frozen. It will make it much easier and faster for the day of the event. All products that you freeze must be taken out of the freezer the day before. Keep them outside for a couple of hours so they are partially defrosted, and put them into a regular refrigerator between 38 and 40 degrees. In the summer, between 36 and 38 degrees is preferred. The menu I will present to you will be easy to make—of course, with some help—and you will not be embarrassed by the quality of food and presentation.

It is preferred that you make a few items on the day of the event, such as hot sauce and rice. And of course, only hot vegetables should be on your menu.

For any menus you're going to use, you need to have some of the following items:

- italian parsley
- cilantro
- fresh or dried rosemary
- fresh garlic
- peppercorns
- olive oil
- italian seasoning
- salt and pepper
- vegetable oil
- beef and chicken bouillon paste or powder

Most home kitchens have at least half of these items. They are useful for almost anything you plan to prepare.

Keep all spices in one area where you are going to work so you can find what you need immediately. Before you start any preparation, you must ensure that you have all your pots, pans, and aluminum available in the house. You can store them in your garage, but anything you're going to use from the garage must be rinsed out. When you pick and choose your items from the menu, you must make sure you have everything in the house, because it can be really frustrating if you have to stop your work to run to the store.

You have to make one very important note to yourself: do not allow any distractions from friends or anything else. If you focus on preparation properly, you will have a successful menu and a successful event.

Over one hundred full-size menus are available. Each menu is seven to nine courses for dinner, priced from high to low. I will give you a few different options, because we are working under a tight budget, and your limitations at home are very narrow. This doesn't mean that you cannot substitute items or that you can't create your own menu, but anything you do you must remember that you only have $500 budgeted for food expenses.

When purchasing items for the menu, carefully purchase the quantity while watching prices, otherwise you will be over budget. The menus presented are not fancy; however, you can provide a nice, enjoyable catering event with them. Most importantly, you will be able to maintain a budget to accommodate eighty to one hundred people.

Breast of Chicken Sliced and Rolled with Mozzarella Cheese in Lemon Sauce

Ingredients:

Chicken
- 13 to 15 pounds boneless chicken breasts
- 3 pounds shredded mozzarella
- 12 ounces chopped onion
- 1/2 bunch chopped italian parsley
- 5 medium garlic cloves, minced
- black pepper

Sauce
- milk
- 10 ounces margarine
- 2 large onions, chopped
- 1 bunch fresh celery
- 2 tablespoons fresh minced garlic
- 10 ounces white flour
- 2 quarts chicken stock or water
- 2 glasses dry white wine
- 3 tablespoons chicken bouillon
- 3 tablespoons chopped dill
- salt and pepper to taste

Preparation:

1. Preheat oven to 375 degrees. Wash chicken breasts with cold water. Pat dry.
2. Slice each breast into approximately six or seven slices. Spread the slices out on a table and spread with the cheese, onion, parsley, and garlic. Sprinkle with black pepper.
3. Roll each slice tightly and place in a baking pan (you can use a disposable aluminum pan). Brush lightly with olive oil. Bake for 15–20 minutes.

4. While the chicken is baking, prepare the sauce: In a 3- to 4-quart saucepan, combine the milk, margarine, onions, celery, and garlic, and cook until golden brown. Add the flour and continue to stir. Add the stock and wine. Continue to stir over medium heat until thick and smooth. Add the bouillon, dill, salt, and pepper. Reduce heat to low and simmer.

5. Pour sauce onto chicken, cover, and heat for approximately 45 minutes.

Tip: You can prepare the chicken a couple of weeks prior to the event. Pull out of the freezer the night before the event and keep refrigerated.

Approximate cost: $55 to $60

Mediterranean Skewers

Ingredients:
- 6 pounds ground beef
- 1 cup bread crumbs
- 3 eggs
- 2 tablespoons garlic
- salt and black pepper
- 1 large bunch italian parsley
- 6 large green peppers, cubed
- 6 large onions, cubed
- 1 pint cherry tomatoes, washed
- 7 pounds italian sausage, cut into 3/4-inch slices
- crushed red pepper (optional)
- olive oil
- 1 package medium skewers (100 count)

Preparation:
1. Preheat oven to 400 degrees. Place ground beef in a mixing bowl. Add the bread crumbs, eggs, garlic, salt, pepper, and half the parsley. Mix well. Roll into 1/2- to 3/4-inch meatballs.
2. On each skewer, evenly skewer pepper cubes, onion cubes, tomatoes, sausage slices, and meatballs. Spread skewers out evenly on a baking pan. Sprinkle with crushed red pepper.

3. Bake for approximately 25 minutes, or maybe grill.

Tip: The skewers can be prepared through the end of step 2 a couple of weeks prior to the event and frozen. Defrost in the fridge the night before.

Approximate cost: $67

Beef Wrapped with Wild Rice and Bacon

Ingredients:
- 6 pounds eye round
- 1 large onion, chopped
- 4 stalks celery, chopped
- 2 tablespoons minced garlic
- 1/2 cup vegetable or olive oil
- 3 cups brown or white rice, cooked
- 2 large eggs
- 1/2 cup bread crumbs
- 2 tablespoons oregano
- salt and pepper
- 2 pounds bacon, sliced thin, each slice cut into three strips

Sauce
- 1/4 cup olive or vegetable oil
- 1 medium onion, chopped
- 1 tablespoon chopped garlic
- 1 orange, chopped with skin
- 1 1/2 cups white flour
- 2 cups burgundy wine
- 1 to 2 tablespoons beef bouillon
- salt and pepper

Preparation:
1. Roast the eye round at 400 degrees for approximately 1 hour 45 minutes. Cool to room temperature. Trim all fat and refrigerate. If you have access to a slicer, slice into thin slices. If not, use a very sharp butcher knife and slice as thin possible.

2. Sauté the onion, celery, and garlic in the oil until golden brown. Add to a mixing bowl with the rice, eggs, bread crumbs, and oregano. Mix well and add salt and pepper to taste.

3. Preheat the oven to 375 degrees. Lay the beef slices flat, place an equal amount of the rice mixture on each slice, and roll tight. Roll a bacon strip tightly around each beef roll.

4. Place the rolls in a baking pan and bake 15 to 20 minutes. Remove from the oven. If there is any juice left from the pan, save it for later.

5. Make the sauce: In 3 quart saucepan, heat the oil, and then add the onion and garlic. Stir until golden. Add the orange and sauté well. Add the flour and stir until golden brown. Add the wine, 1 quart of hot water, the bouillon, and salt and pepper to taste. Stir until smooth and thickened.

6. Pour the sauce on the beef and bake 30 to 40 minutes at 375 to 400 degrees.

Tip: Although the beef rolls can be prepared through step 4 in advance, the sauce must be made the day of the event.

Approximate cost: $65

Stuffed Marinated Mushrooms with Shrimp

Ingredients:
- 80–100 medium mushrooms
- juice of 2 large lemons
- salt and pepper to taste

Filling
- 32 ounces chopped baby shrimp
- 1 lemon rind, grated
- 1 tablespoon chopped basil
- 3 large celery stalks, chopped fine
- 1 medium red pepper, chopped
- 1 tablespoon minced garlic

- 1/2 cup olive oil
- 3/4 cup lemon juice

For serving
- spinach leaves
- 1 bunch italian parsley, chopped
- 3 tablespoons shredded lemon skins

Preparation:

1. Soak the mushrooms in cold water. Remove stems. Toss with both hands in a mixing bowl, and then wash again.
2. Place the mushrooms in a clean bowl. Pour the lemon juice over. Add salt and pepper to taste.
3. Prepare the filling: In a bowl, combine the chopped shrimp with the remaining filling ingredients. Mix well.
4. To serve, place spinach leaves on the bottom of trays. Place mushrooms on top of the spinach leaves. Fill each mushroom with shrimp mix. Sprinkle the parsley and lemon skins on top.

Tip: You can prepare this appetizer three days before the event. Keep covered and refrigerated.

Approximate cost: $???????????

Melon Wedges Wrapped with Smoked Ham

Ingredients:
- julienned lettuce, for serving
- 5 medium cantaloupes, peeled, cleaned, halved, and sliced into equal wedges (each melon half should yield approximately 10 wedges)
- 3 pounds thin-sliced smoked ham
- 1 medium carrot, grated

Dressing
- 10 ounces balsamic vinegar
- 4 ounces olive oil
- 2 scallions, chopped fine

- 2 tablespoons chopped fresh dill
- 1 1/2 tablespoons sugar
- 1 tablespoon minced garlic
- salt and pepper to taste

Preparation:

1. Spread julienned lettuce on a tray. Place cantaloupe wedges atop the lettuce. Wrap smoked ham around the wedges.
2. Combine the dressing ingredients and mix well. With a spoon, lightly drizzle the dressing over the top of the melon and ham. Scatter grated carrot over.

Tip: This appetizer can be prepared two days prior to the event.

Approximate cost: $30

Smoked Salmon on Mini Garlic Toast

Ingredients:

- 2 french baguettes, sliced 1/8 inch thick
- 10 ounces melted butter
- 24 ounces sliced smoked salmon

Cream-cheese mixture

- 4 pounds cream cheese
- 1/4 cup milk
- 2 tablespoons sweet paprika
- 2 tablespoons chopped parsley
- 1 tablespoon minced garlic
- juice of 1 lemon

For serving

- 3 tablespoons grated lime skin
- 1/4 cup fresh parsley chopped
- 1 tablespoon sweet paprika
- 6 round doilies

Preparation:

1. Preheat oven to 350 degrees. Place baguette slices on a baking sheet, brush each side with butter, and bake until golden brown.
2. Mix the ingredients for the cream-cheese mixture in a blender or mixing bowl. Place into a piping bag (medium tube) and pipe mixture equally onto center of each baguette slice.
3. Place a thin strip of salmon on top of the cream-cheese mixture (cutting as needed to conserve).
4. Place doilies on a serving tray. Place baguette slices on the doilies. Sprinkle with the lime skin, parsley, and sweet paprika.

Tip: This appetizer may be prepared two days prior to the event. Refrigerate and cover top lightly (be careful not to smash).

Approximate cost: $40

Multicolor Pasta Salad

Ingredients:

Salad

- 5 (12-ounce) boxes multicolor pasta
- 2 pounds fresh broccoli, chopped
- 1 pound spinach leaves
- 1 red onion, julienne sliced
- 1 bunch italian parsley
- 1 medium carrot, grated
- 3 tablespoons minced garlic
- 12–16 ounces balsamic vinegar
- salt and pepper to taste
- 1 tablespoon nutmeg

For serving

- 7 or 8 romaine lettuce leaves
- 1 orange, cut into half-moon slices

Preparation:

1. Cook the pasta in a pot of boiling water for 10–12 minutes. Drain and cool with cold water.
2. In a large mixing bowl, combine the pasta with the remaining salad ingredients. Mix gently (to avoid breaking the pasta). Season to taste.
3. Place lettuce leaves around the inside of a glass bowl. Pour the pasta salad into the bowl. Garnish with orange slices.

Approximate cost: $20

Red-Skin Potato Salad

Ingredients:

Salad

- 15 pounds red-skin potatoes (do not peel), boiled, cooled, and cut into small wedges
- 2 bunches scallions, chopped
- 1/2 cup chopped fresh cilantro
- 4 sticks celery, chopped
- 2 large pickles, cubed
- 3 tablespoons chopped garlic
- 12 ounces white vinegar
- 12–16 ounces olive or vegetable oil
- salt and pepper to taste

For serving

- 8 leaves lettuce
- 10 hard-boiled eggs, peeled and halved
- parsley
- 2 tablespoons sweet paprika
- salt and pepper to taste

Preparation:

1. In a mixing bowl, combine the salad ingredients and mix gently with both hands from the bottom upward. Add more vinegar or spices if you like.

2. Line the bottom of a tray with lettuce leaves, with the leaves curving upward to the top. Arrange the potato salad atop the lettuce leaves and add the eggs evenly across tray. Sprinkle with parsley, paprika, salt, and pepper.

Approximate cost: $18

Mini Cold-Cut Rolls

Ingredients:
- 120 mini rolls (firm preferred)
- 2 cups mayonnaise
- 2 heads romaine lettuce, washed
- 2 pounds sliced ham
- 2 pounds sliced smoked turkey
- 2 pounds sliced roast beef
- 4 large tomatoes, washed and sliced thin
- 3 large cucumbers, washed and sliced thin
- 4 large pickles, sliced thin
- 2 pounds provolone or other cheese, sliced thin
- 16 ounces black or green olives
- parsley

Preparation:
1. Cut rolls in half and lay on table. Spread a touch of mayonnaise on each. Distribute the lettuce and 1/2 slice of each meat evenly on the bottoms of the rolls. Add the tomato, cucumber, pickle, and cheese slices. Place the top halves on each roll. Stick a large toothpick through the center. Stick an olive on top of each toothpick.
2. Place doilies on a tray and display the cold-cut rolls on top. Sprinkle with parsley.

Tip: This appetizer is time-consuming to prepare. Assemble three days prior to or preferably the day before the event. Wrap and keep refrigerated.

Approximate cost: $45

Stuffed Baby Tomatoes with Feta and Spinach

Ingredients:
- lettuce leaves
- 50 campari tomatoes, washed, halved, and scooped out
- 1/2 cup chopped fresh parsley

Filling
- 32 ounces crumbled feta cheese
- 1 pound fresh spinach leaves, chopped
- 1 small red onion, chopped fine
- 2 celery stalks, chopped
- 1/2 cup olive oil
- juice of 2 fresh large lemons
- 1 tablespoon grated lemon rind
- 1 tablespoon minced garlic
- 1 tablespoon chopped tarragon
- salt and pepper to taste

Preparation:
1. Spread the lettuce leaves evenly across a tray. Place the tomato halves evenly over tray atop the lettuce.
2. In a bowl, combine the filling ingredients and mix well.
3. Fill the tomatoes equally. Sprinkle with the parsley. Wrap and refrigerate.

Tip: This appetizer may be prepared two days prior to the event.

Approximate cost: $30

Dessert: Peach Cobbler

Ingredients:
- shortening, for greasing pans
- 5 vanilla cake mixes
- 15 eggs
- 2 1/2 cups oil
- 5 cups water
- 11 ounces canned or fresh peaches, strained

- 1 pound fresh cherries, pitted
- 1/2 cup powdered sugar

Preparation:
1. Preheat the oven to 350 degrees. Grease the bottom and inside of two large pans with shortening.
2. In a large bowl, stir together the cake mixes, eggs, oil, and water.
3. Pour mix equally into pans. Sprinkle peaches and cherries evenly into the pans. Bake 30–35 minutes.
4. Cut the cobbler into squares. Place on trays and sprinkle powdered sugar over the top before serving.

Tip: The cobbler may be served hot or cold.

Approximate cost: $18 to $20

Menu #2: Simple Outdoor Grill Menu

Grilled Pork Loin

Ingredients:
- 15 to 16 pounds pork loin, sliced

Marinade
- mustard
- 1 cup olive or vegetable oil
- salt and pepper to taste
- 2 to 3 tablespoons fresh oregano
- 3 tablespoons minced garlic
- 1 large onion, chopped fine
- 1 cup balsamic dressing
- 1/2 cup worcestershire sauce

Preparation:
1. In a bowl, mix the marinade ingredients together.
2. Spread the pork slices out on a pan. Pour marinade over them. Cover and refrigerate. Allow the marinade to penetrate for a couple of hours.
3. Place on the grill 30 minutes prior to serving.

Tip: This dish may be prepared two days prior to grilling. Make sure that the expiration date on the package of meat does not exceed the day of usage.

Approximate cost: $70

Grilled Chicken

Ingredients:
- 10 chickens, cut into ten pieces each

Marinade
- 4 cups dry white wine
- 4 cups barbecue sauce
- 4 tablespoons minced garlic
- salt and pepper to taste
- 1 bunch parsley
- 1 large onion, cut into strips

Preparation:
1. Place the chicken in a bowl. In a separate bowl, mix the marinade well and pour over chicken. Coat well. Cover and refrigerate.
2. Grill the chicken 40 minutes prior to serving on medium-low heat.

Tip: The chicken may be prepared two days prior to grilling. Make sure that the expiration date on the package of chicken does not exceed the day of usage.

Approximate cost: $65

Burger Kebabs

Ingredients:
- 7–10 pounds ground beef
- 1 large onion, chopped
- 1 green pepper, chopped
- 1 bunch parsley, chopped
- 4 tablespoons minced garlic

- 1 cup bread crumbs
- 2 eggs

Preparation:

1. In a large bowl, mix all ingredients well. Roll into finger-sized 2-inch kebabs and refrigerate, covered.
2. Cook on a low to medium grill for approximately 25 minutes.

Tip: The kebabs may be prepared and placed into deep-freeze two weeks prior to the event.

Approximate cost: $45

Baked Potatoes

Ingredients:

- 80–100 medium-sized potatoes
- olive oil, for brushing
- salt

Topping

- 32 ounces sour cream
- 32 ounces shredded cheddar cheese
- 2 large onions, chopped
- 1 cup chives

Preparation:

1. Preheat oven to 400 degrees. Poke potatoes with a fork. Brush with olive oil and salt. Wrap individually with foil.
2. Bake the potatoes for approximately 1 hour. Alternatively, place on grill or into fire pit. Poke with a skewer to check when full cooked.
3. Mix together the topping ingredients and serve alongside the potatoes.

Approximate cost: $35

Corn on the Cob

Ingredients:
- 80–100 (4-inch) corncobs
- 32 ounces butter
- sea salt

Preparation:
1. Place corn into a large pot. Bring to a boil. Reduce to simmer. Keep in water until serving time.
2. Melt the butter. Just before serving, place corn into a serving dish and pour butter over it. Sprinkle with sea salt.

Tip: Instead of boiling, you can wrap the corncobs individually in foil and place into a fire pit for grilling, if you have enough space.

Approximate cost:

Homemade Baked Beans

Ingredients:
- 2 large onions, chopped
- 8 medium carrots, cut into 1-inch slices
- 1 bunch parsley, chopped
- 10 potatoes
- 6 pounds dried beans of your choice, washed
- 2 pounds pork, beef, or bacon, cubed
- 3 cups ketchup
- 1 cup mustard
- 1 cup dark brown sugar
- 1 cup beef bouillon
- 1/4 cup chopped garlic
- salt and pepper to taste

Preparation:
1. In a large electric Crock-Pot, sauté the onions, carrots, parsley, potatoes, and garlic in oil until golden.

2. Add the beans to the Crock-Pot. Add the remaining ingredients. Add boiling water until 3/4 full. Cover and cook on high, mixing occasionally, until simmering. Place on low heat and cook overnight. If necessary, add more liquid during the cooking process or before serving.

Tip: If you don't have an electric Crock-Pot, you can make this recipe with two Crock-Pots on the stove. Divide the ingredients evenly between them.

Approximate cost: $35

Garden Salad

Ingredients:
- 7 heads romaine lettuce, washed and patted dry, cut into approximately 1/2-inch slices
- 3 large carrots, grated
- 2 medium-sized red onions, sliced
- 2 large cucumbers, sliced
- 2 large red peppers, sliced

Oil and vinegar dressing
- 2 cups balsamic vinegar
- 1 1/2 cups olive oil
- 1 cup cold water
- 3 tablespoons minced garlic
- 3 tablespoons sugar
- 2 tablespoons fresh oregano
- salt and pepper to taste

Creamy dressing
- 3 cups mayonnaise
- 1/2 cup vinegar
- 1/2 cup lemon juice
- 1/2 cup parmesan cheese
- 1/2 cup milk or half-and-half
- 1 carrot, grated fine

- 2 tablespoons minced garlic
- 2 tablespoons of dill
- salt and pepper to taste

Preparation:
1. Arrange the lettuce on a tray. Sprinkle the remaining vegetables on top.
2. In separate bowls, combine the ingredients for each of the dressings. Mix well.
3. Place dressings in serving bowls with ladles. Serve beside the salad.

Approximate cost: $20–$25

Fruit Salad

Ingredients:
- 1 large seedless watermelon, peeled and cubed
- 4 cantaloupes, peeled and cubed
- 1 honeydew, peeled and cubed
- 1 pineapple, peeled and cubed
- 1 pint blueberries
- 3 pounds strawberries, trimmed
- red or green grapes
- lettuce, for serving (optional)
- 2 cups orange juice
- 1 cup lemon juice

Preparation:
1. Place all the fruit in a large bowl lined with lettuce, or into a bowl or on a tray with edges.
2. Pour orange and lemon juice over the fruit. Wrap and refrigerate.

Tip: The salad may be prepared two days prior to the event.

Approximate cost: $35–$40

Chopped Mediterranean Salad

Ingredients:
- 8 large tomatoes, washed and cubed
- 5 large cucumbers, washed and cubed
- 4 large green peppers, washed and cubed
- 1 small red cabbage, washed and cubed
- 6 scallions, sliced
- 1 1/2 cup lemon juice
- 1 1/2 cup olive oil
- 1 bunch of italian parsley, chopped
- 4 tablespoons minced garlic
- 1/4 cup chopped fresh oregano
- 1 fresh jalapeño pepper, chopped (optional)

Preparation:
1. In a bowl, combine the tomatoes, cucumbers, green peppers, cabbage, and scallions. Add the lemon juice, olive oil, parsley, garlic, oregano, and jalapeño. Gently mix.
2. Place the salad onto a serving platter with edges or a serving bowl.

Tip: If this is prepared two days prior to event, add the spices and dressing right before serving.

Approximate cost: $35

Hummus and Pita

Ingredients:
- 2 large cans (120 ounces) garbanzo beans, strained
- 2 1/2 cups olive oil
- 1 1/2 cups fresh lemon juice
- salt and pepper to taste
- 1/4 cup minced garlic
- 1 tablespoon saffron

For serving
- lettuce
- parsley
- pita

Preparation:
1. In a mixing bowl, smash the beans with your hands.
2. Add remaining the ingredients and mix well. Season to taste. May be prepared spicy.
3. Put the hummus into serving bowl or platter with lettuce-covered edges. Sprinkle with parsley. Serve with pita bread.

Tip: The hummus must be made two days prior to the event.

Approximate cost: $25–$30

Tomato Mozzarella Salad

Ingredients:
- 14 large tomatoes, washed, stems removed, halved, and sliced
- lettuce
- 4 pounds fresh mozzarella
- parsley

Dressing
- 2 cups sour cream
- 1 cup poppy seeds
- 3/4 cup lemon juice
- 1/2 cup olive oil
- 2 stalks celery, chopped
- 3 tablespoons fresh chopped dill
- 1 tablespoon fresh garlic

Preparation:
1. Place the tomato slices on a tray padded with lettuce, stacked like steps.
2. Make the dressing: In a mixing bowl, combine all the dressing ingredients. Mix well. Pour onto tomatoes before serving.

3. Place thin strips of mozzarella on top of the tomatoes and sprinkle with parsley. Wrap and refrigerate until serving.

Tip: You can prepare this two days prior to the event. Do not pour dressing on until serving.

Approximate cost $30–$35

Dessert: Spumoni

Ingredients:
- 3 chocolate cake mixes
- 3 vanilla cake mixes
- 1 cup rum
- 1 quart liquid whipping cream
- 2 cups melted chocolate
- 2 cans condensed evaporated milk
- 12 ounces cherry pie filling
- 2 cups sliced strawberries
- 1 cup maraschino cherries

Preparation:
1. Bake the cake mixes according to box directions. When cooled, crumble an equal portion of each cake into a glass bowl. Pour rum over cakes to taste.
2. Whip the whipping cream. Place a layer over the cake in the bowl.
3. Mix the chocolate and condensed milk together. Pour lightly over the whipped cream. Add on a second layer of whipped cream and chocolate.
4. Add a layer of cherry pie filling to the bowl and top with a layer of whipped cream. Add another layer of chocolate, whipped cream, and rum.
5. Add the remaining cake and the remaining rum. Top with the remaining whipped cream and the strawberries.
6. Place the maraschino cherries around the bowl. If necessary, you add more chocolate on top of the strawberries. Wrap and refrigerate until serving.

Tip: The dessert can be prepared three to four days prior to the event.

Approximate cost: $40

Menu #3

- Beef Burgundy
- Stuffed Flounder with Crab Florentine
- Chicken Scampi
- Roasted Red-Skin Potatoes
- Brown or White Rice
- Zucchini and Red Pepper
- Cucumber Salad
- Marinated Red Cabbage
- Watermelon with Feta Cheese
- Dinner Rolls with Butter
- Stuffed Baked Apples
- Fresh-Fruit-Blend Punch
- Homemade Iced Tea
- Water
- Coffee

Beef Burgundy

Ingredients:
- 16 ounces margarine, divided
- 2 large onions, chopped into large pieces
- 10–12 pounds beef top round, cut into cubes and washed
- 4 cups burgundy wine
- 1 1/2 cup white flour
- salt and pepper to taste
- 2 large green peppers
- 3 tablespoons minced garlic
- 3 tablespoons beef bouillon

Preparation:

1. Melt 8 ounces of the margarine in large pot. Add the onions and sauté. Add the beef and stir. Cook 10–15 minutes.
2. Add the burgundy and stir on medium heat for a few minutes.
3. Add 6 quarts of boiling water. Bring to a boil. Skim foam from top. Cover. Reduce to medium heat. Cook approximately 1 1/2 hours (adding water as necessary when the beef is nearly done). Remove the beef and set aside, reserving the cooking liquid.
4. Place another pot on the stove and add the remaining margarine. Add the flour and stir until browned. Add the liquid from the beef (approximately 2 1/2 quarts). Add the burgundy. Whisk well until blended.
5. Add the meat. Season with salt and pepper. Simmer and stir occasionally and gently for 15 to 20 minutes until ready to serve.

Tip: The dish can be prepared two days prior to event. Reheat in a 350-degree oven or on a stovetop over low heat.

Approximate cost: $80

Stuffed Flounder with Crab Florentine

Ingredients:
*   1/2 cup olive oil
*   1 bundle celery, chopped
*   1 medium onion, chopped
*   2 pounds crabmeat (claw is okay)
*   2 pounds fresh spinach leaves
*   eggs
*   1 cup seasoned bread crumbs
*   1 cup shredded mozzarella cheese
*   2 tablespoons Old Bay seasoning
*   50 medium pieces flounder fillets

Dressing
*   1 1/2 cups lemon juice
*   1 pound butter or margarine

- 2 tablespoons chopped mint
- salt and pepper to taste

Preparation:
1. In large saucepan, heat the olive oil. Add the celery and onion. Stir until golden brown. Add the crabmeat. Remove from stove and cool to room temperature.
2. Add the spinach, eggs, bread crumbs, mozzarella, and Old Bay seasoning to the crabmeat mixture. Mix well.
3. Preheat oven to 375 degrees. Spread out the flounder fillets. Cut each fillet in half. Place about 1 tablespoon of the crabmeat mixture in the center of each fillet. Roll and place on a baking sheet with edges. Bake for 15–20 minutes.
4. In a pan, combine all dressing ingredients until the butter is melted. Pour over fillets. Heat an extra 10 minutes.

Tip: This dish may be prepared two weeks ahead. Wrap and place in a deep freezer. Do not add the dressing until reheating for usage. Thaw fillets in the fridge the night before reheating.

Approximate cost: $70

Chicken Scampi

Ingredients:
- 1 cup olive oil
- 2 large onions, sliced
- 2 heads celery, chopped fine
- 8 medium carrots, cut into cubes
- 4 tablespoons chopped garlic
- 14 pounds boneless chicken breasts, trimmed, washed, and cut into thin strips
- 36 ounces white wine
- salt and pepper to taste
- 16 ounces margarine
- 2 1/2 cups white flour
- 4 portobello mushrooms or other mushrooms

- 3 tablespoons chicken bouillon or chicken stock
- 1 cup chopped italian parsley, for garnish

Preparation:
1. Preheat the oven to 400 degrees.
2. In a large pan, heat the olive oil. Add the onions, celery, carrots, and garlic. Sauté 5 to 6 minutes.
3. Add the chicken and sauté 10–15 minutes. Add the wine, salt, and pepper.
4. Place the chicken mixture into a baking dish and bake for 15–20 minutes.
5. In large pan, heat the margarine and flour until golden brown. Add 2 1/2–3 quarts boiling water. Stir until blended. Add salt and pepper. Pour onto the chicken.
6. Continue to bake the chicken for 40 minutes more. When ready to serve, sprinkle the italian parsley on top for garnish.

Tip: May be prepared a day prior to serving. Reheat in a 400-degree oven for ????? minutes.

Approximate cost: $70

Roasted Red-Skin Potatoes

Ingredients:
- 20 pounds red-skin potatoes, boiled and cooled
- onion
- salt and pepper to taste
- 2 cups olive oil
- 1 cup chopped parsley

Preparation:
1. Preheat the oven to 400 degrees.
2. Slice each potato into 2–5 slices. Stack like steps across an aluminum baking pan (disposable is fine). On each layer, sprinkle onion, salt, and pepper. Make a double layer in each pan. Divide evenly among the pans.

3. Pour the olive oil evenly over the potato slices and sprinkle parsley over the top.

4. Wrap with foil and bake for approximately one hour.

Tip: May be prepared two days prior to the event. If prepared two weeks prior, the potatoes may be frozen. Remove from the freezer one day prior to usage. (Heating time will vary, but plan on approximately 1 1/2 hours). Do not put the oil and parsley on the potatoes until day of serving.

Approximate cost: $27

Brown or White Rice

Ingredients:
- 1 cup vegetable or olive oil
- 1 large onion, chopped
- 4 stalks celery, chopped
- 2 large carrots, grated
- 1 bunch parsley, chopped, plus more for garnish
- 2 1/2 quarts brown or white rice
- 1 tablespoon minced garlic
- salt and pepper to taste
- 4 tablespoons beef or chicken bouillon

Preparation:
1. Heat the oil in an approximately 10-quart pan. Add the onion, celery, carrots, and parsley. Sauté for 5 minutes.

2. Add the rice, garlic, salt, and pepper. Stir consistently over medium heat until golden brown.

3. Pour 5 quarts boiling water (1 quart extra for brown rice) into the rice and stir. Add bouillon and season to taste. Boil approximately 1 minute. Reduce to a simmer and cover tightly. Cook 20–25 minutes for white rice and approximately 40 minutes for brown rice.

4. When ready to serve, fluff the rice and place in a serving pan. Garnish with a sprinkle of parsley.

Tip: The rice may be prepared and frozen two weeks prior to the event. Divide into three to four large ziplock bags. Reheat, covered, in microwave or in oven at 350 degrees for 1 1/2 hours.

Approximate cost: $25

Zucchini and Red Pepper

Ingredients:
- 15 large zucchini, washed and cut lengthwise into 1/2-inch wedges
- 4 large red peppers, washed and cut into wedges
- 3 medium-sized red onions, julienned
- 1 cup white wine

Marinade
- 12 ounces olive oil
- 12 ounces lemon juice
- 1/2 cup chopped rosemary
- 5 tablespoons garlic, minced
- 3 tablespoons fresh oregano (dry is okay)
- 1 lemon rind, grated
- salt and pepper

Garnish
- 1 quart chopped spinach
- 2 large tomatoes, tomatoes

Preparation:
1. Place the zucchini and red peppers into a baking pan (disposable aluminum is okay).
2. Add all marinade ingredients and mix well.
3. Place under broiler for approximately 25 to 30 minutes.

Approximate cost: $35

Cucumber Salad

Ingredients:

Salad
- 12 large cucumbers, sliced thin
- 2 medium red onions, sliced into rounds
- 1 pound kalamata olives
- 1 tablespoon garlic
- 1 1/2 cup red wine vinegar
- 1 1/2 olive oil
- salt and pepper to taste

For serving
- 8 leaves romaine lettuce
- 1/2 cup cilantro
- 2 large oranges, sliced into rounds

Preparation:
1. In a mixing bowl, combine all the salad ingredients and mix gently.
2. Place the lettuce leaves into a serving bowl or platter. Serve the cucumbers on the lettuce. Sprinkle with cilantro. Place orange slices around edges.

Tip: Can be made one day prior to the event.

Approximate cost: $30

Marinated Red Cabbage

Ingredients:

Cabbage
- 4 large heads red cabbage, washed, halved, and cored
- 4 large carrots, grated
- 1 1/2 cups olive oil
- 1 1/2 cups white vinegar or cider vinegar
- 1/2 cup sugar

- salt and pepper to taste
- 2 lime rinds, grated

For serving
- julienned lettuce strips, for decoration
- 1/2 cup chopped fresh parsley, for garnish

Preparation:
1. Cut each cabbage half into thirds. Shred with a sharp knife.
2. Place the cabbage into a large bowl and add the remaining ingredients. Mix well. Adjust flavor to taste. Place into large salad bowl or large tray with thick edge.
3. Place thin julienned lettuce strips around the tray edges and sprinkle with the parsley.

Tip: The cabbage may be prepared two days prior to the event, but I recommend preparing it on event day.

Approximate cost: $20

Watermelon with Feta Cheese

Ingredients:
- 8 leaves lettuce
- 1 medium seedless watermelon, peeled and cut into cubes
- 2 pounds crumbled feta cheese
- 1/2 cup balsamic dressing
- 1 cup olive oil
- salt and pepper to taste
- 1 cup julienned fresh spinach
- 1/2 cup shocked mint leaves

Preparation:
1. Place the lettuce on a serving tray. Arrange the watermelon cubes on top of the lettuce. Sprinkle with feta cheese.
2. In a bowl, combine the balsamic dressing, olive oil, salt, and pepper.

3. Sprinkle the spinach and mint over the watermelon. Pour the dressing on just before serving.

Tip: Watermelon and dressing may be prepared, separately, two days prior.

Approximate cost: $30

Menu #4: Vegetarian

- Assorted Vegetarian Quiches
- Stuffed Avocado Halves
- Puff Pastry Filled with Potato and Spinach
- Red-Skin Potatoes Stuffed with Broccoli, Celery, and Onion
- Roma Tomato Halves Stuffed with Fish
- Exotic Tuna Salad
- Deviled Eggs Stuffed with Cream Cheese and Salmon
- Pasta Salad
- Fresh Spinach-Leaf Salad
- Fresh Marinated Green Bean Salad
- Baked Macaroni-and-Cheese Squares
- Fresh Beet Salad
- Dessert: Pear Compote

Approximate cost: $350 to $400

This menu is very practical for summertime outdoor events.

Assorted Vegetarian Quiches

Ingredients:
- 10 shallow pie shells
- 1/2 cup olive oil
- 2 large onions, chopped
- 2 tablespoons minced garlic
- 32–40 ounces cooked broccoli, chopped
- 6 large tomatoes, cubed
- 15 eggs
- 1 quart whole milk

- 1 bunch italian parsley
- salt and pepper to taste
- 36 ounces mozzarella cheese

Preparation:
1. Preheat oven to 375 degrees. Prick or pierce pie shells with a fork. Heat in oven 5 to 6 minutes. Remove and cool. Leave oven on.
2. In large sauté pan, heat the oil and then sauté the onions and garlic until golden brown.
3. Spread the broccoli in the pie shells. Add the tomatoes, onions, and garlic.
4. In a mixing bowl, beat together the eggs, milk, parsley, salt, pepper, and cheese. Pour equally into the pie shells.
5. Place the quiches on a baking sheet and bake for 25–35 minutes. Remove from oven and let cool.

Tip: The quiches may be baked and frozen two to three weeks prior to the event. If frozen, thaw in the refrigerator the night before the event. Reheat in a 375-degree oven for 35–40 minutes, lightly covered with parchment paper or foil.

Approximate cost:

Stuffed Avocado Halves

Ingredients:
- 40 to 50 medium avocados (not mushy or hard), halved and pitted
- 12 ounces lemon juice
- lettuce
- celery, chopped
- tomatoes, cut into wedges
- 1 fresh lemon rind, grated small

Filling
- 96 ounces white cheddar, shredded
- 36 ounces cream cheese, whipped
- 1 pound spinach leaves, julienned

- 4 medium chopped sweet red peppers
- 6–7 scallions, chopped
- 10 ounces olive oil
- 4 tablespoons garlic, minced
- salt and pepper to taste
- dash of rosemary

Dressing
- 1/3 cup vinegar
- 1/3 cup olive oil
- 1/3 cup water
- spoonful of sugar
- salt and pepper to taste

Preparation:
1. Carefully scrape the avocados from their shells into a mixing bowl. Pour lemon juice over to preserve the color. Place the avocado shells on a tray covered with lettuce.
2. Add the filling ingredients to the avocado in the mixing bowl. Mix ingredients together with a mixer or by hand.
3. Fill the avocado shells equally with the avocado mixture. Sprinkle with chopped celery. Place a tomato wedge on top of each.
4. Combine all the dressing ingredients and mix well. Pour over the stuffed avocados just before serving.

Approximate cost:

Puff Pastry Filled with Potato and Spinach

Ingredients:
- 8 ounces olive oil
- 2 large onions, chopped
- 4 celery stalks, chopped
- 4 tablespoons minced garlic
- 10 pounds red-skin potatoes with skin, cooked and chopped
- 8 eggs
- 1 cup mozzarella or swiss cheese

- 1 pound fresh spinach leaves
- salt and pepper to taste
- 5 packages phyllo dough or 10 pounds puff pastry dough

Preparation:

1. Preheat the oven to 375 degrees.
2. In a large sauté pan, heat the oil. Add the onions, celery, and garlic, and sauté 5–6 minutes. Remove from stove.
3. In a mixing bowl, combine the potatoes with the sautéed vegetables. Add four of the eggs along with the cheese, spinach, salt, and pepper. Mix well.
4. Combine four pieces of phyllo for each roll. In a bowl, beat the remaining four eggs. With a pastry brush, brush the phyllo dough with the beaten eggs.
5. Place the filling along one edge of each piece of dough. Roll several times until sealed well. Place on baking sheets greased with shortening or oil, spaced approximately 1 1/2 inches apart. Cut approximately 2 1/2-inch slits into the rolls with a knife.
6. Bake the rolls for 20–25 minutes. Remove from oven. Cool. Separate into pieces where the slits are.
7. Place the rolls onto a steel serving tray. Reheat 15 minutes prior to use, or eat at room temperature.

Tip: The pastries may be prepared three to four weeks ahead of time.

Approximate cost:

Red-Skin Potatoes Stuffed with Broccoli, Celery, and Onion

Ingredients:

- 50 medium red-skin potatoes, boiled and halved
- 8 ounces olive oil
- 1 large onion, chopped
- 5 celery sticks, chopped
- 2 tablespoons minced garlic
- 5 pounds cooked broccoli, chopped
- salt and pepper to taste

- 3 large eggs
- 2 cups shredded mozzarella cheese
- 1 1/2 cups bread crumbs
- 1 cup italian parsley, chopped

Preparation:

1. Preheat the oven to 375 degrees. Carefully scoop the centers out of the potatoes into a mixing bowl. Place the skins onto a baking sheet.
2. In a pan, heat the oil and sauté the onion, celery, and garlic. After 4–5 minutes, add the broccoli, salt, and pepper. Remove from the stove.
3. Add the sautéed vegetables to the mixing bowl with the potatoes. Add the eggs, cheese, bread crumbs, and parsley. Gently mix well.
4. Fill each potato skin equally with the potato mixture. Bake for approximately 40 minutes, until a light, crunchy crust forms on top.

Tip: The potatoes be prepared three to four weeks ahead and frozen. To reheat, bake at 350 degrees for one hour. Cover if necessary.

Approximate cost:

Roma Tomato Halves Stuffed with Fish

Ingredients:

- 50 medium Roma tomatoes, halved and scooped
- 4 pounds cooked fish (flounder, tilapia, cod, mahimahi, or tuna)
- 8 ounces olive oil
- 1 medium red onion, chopped
- 5 stalks celery, chopped
- 4 large carrots, grated and cooked
- 2 lemons, rinds grated
- 3 tablespoons minced garlic
- 2 medium zucchini, grated
- 1 egg
- 1 1/2 cups bread crumbs
- 1 1/2 cups cheddar cheese

- salt and pepper to taste
- fresh dill, for serving
- 4 stalks scallions, chopped

Preparation:

1. Preheat oven to 375 degrees. Place tomato halves onto a lightly greased baking pan. In a mixing bowl, break up the fish.
2. In a sauté pan, heat the oil and sauté the onion, celery, carrots, lemon rind, and garlic for 4 to 5 minutes. Pour into fish. Add the zucchini, egg, bread crumbs, cheese, salt, and pepper. Gently mix well (do not mush together).
3. Fill the tomato halves equally with the fish mixture. Bake 15–20 minutes.
4. Place tomatoes on a steel pan. Before serving, sprinkle with fresh dill. Halve the lemons and squeeze juice on top.

Tip: May be eaten hot or cold.

Approximate cost:

Exotic Tuna Salad

Ingredients:

Salad

- 64 ounces tuna in water, drained and squeezed, or fresh grilled tuna
- 10 stalks celery, chopped fine
- 4 large scallions, chopped
- 4 large carrots, grated
- 5 large persimmons, peeled and chopped
- 1 cup italian parsley
- 36 ounces mayonnaise
- salt and pepper to taste

For serving

- thinly sliced limes
- paprika
- chopped parsley

Preparation:

1. Combine all salad ingredients in a bowl and mix gently.
2. Place salad on a serving tray covered with lettuce leaves. Smooth with a spatula, creating a 1-inch-high edge. Decorate with the limes. Sprinkle with paprika and chopped parsley.

Approximate cost:

Deviled Eggs Stuffed with Cream Cheese and Salmon

Ingredients:

- 50 hard-boiled eggs, peeled and halved
- 2 pounds cream cheese, whipped
- 1/4 pound smoked salmon, chopped
- 8–10 ounces mayonnaise
- 1 tablespoon mustard
- salt and pepper to taste

For serving

- lettuce leaves
- round crackers
- paprika
- 1/4 cup parsley

Preparation:

1. Carefully remove the egg yolks from the whites. Place the yolks in a mixing bowl. Place the whites on a serving tray covered with lettuce.
2. Add the cream cheese, smoked salmon, mayonnaise, mustard, salt, and pepper to the bowl with the egg yolks. Beat on high speed until smooth.
3. Fill a large-tipped piping bag with the salmon mixture and pipe equally into each egg-white half. Garnish with round crackers topped lengthwise onto each egg. Sprinkle with paprika and parsley.

Tip: May be made two days prior to serving.

Approximate cost:

Pasta Salad

Ingredients:

Salad

- 16 ounces tricolor pasta, cooked, chilled 15–20 minutes
- 1 1/2 pounds fresh broccoli, chopped large
- 1 1/2 pounds fresh spinach leaves
- 1 pound kalamata olives
- 1 medium red onion, julienned
- 1 bunch italian parsley, chopped
- 1/4 cup chopped oregano
- salt and pepper to taste

Dressing

- 16 ounces olive oil
- 12 ounces balsamic vinegar
- 3 tablespoons sugar

For serving

- lettuce leaves
- tomatoes, cut into wedges

Preparation:

1. In a large mixing bowl, combine all salad ingredients.
2. In a small mixing bowl, combine the dressing ingredients and mix well.
3. Pour the dressing over the pasta and gently mix well.
4. Place the pasta into a serving salad bowl. Season to taste. Decorate with lettuce leaves and tomato wedges around the lettuce in bowl.

Tip: The salad may be prepared two days prior to the event.

Approximate cost:

Fresh Spinach-Leaf Salad

Ingredients:
- 4 pounds large spinach leaves, washed and dried
- 1 pint cherry tomatoes, washed
- 2 large sweet red peppers, julienned
- 2 large cucumbers, cut into slices
- 1 large red onion, cut thin

Dressing
- 16 ounces olive oil
- 12 ounces lemon juice
- 1 1/2 cups shredded parmesan (canned okay)
- 1/2 cup chopped dill
- 2 tablespoons fresh oregano
- 4 tablespoons sugar
- 4 tablespoons minced garlic
- salt and pepper to taste

Preparation:
1. Place the spinach leaves on two large serving trays. Arrange the tomatoes around the tray. Add the peppers on top of the spinach. Place the cucumber slices around the tray. Sprinkle the onion on top of the peppers.
2. In a mixing bowl, combine all dressing ingredients and mix well. Place into a serving bowl with a ladle. Serve beside the spinach salad.

Tip: The salad and dressing may be prepared two days prior to the event.

Approximate cost:

Fresh Marinated Green Bean Salad

Ingredients:
Salad
- 6 pounds fresh green beans, snapped
- 5 large plums

- 2 large carrots, peeled and grated
- 2 large tomatoes, cubed
- 1 large red onion, julienned
- 1/2 cup chopped mint leaves
- 4 tablespoons garlic, minced
- 12 ounces olive oil
- 12 ounces apple cider or balsamic vinegar
- salt and pepper to taste

For serving
- julienned lettuce
- chopped red pepper

Preparation:
1. Place the green beans into boiling water for four minutes. Cool with cold water.
2. In a mixing bowl, combine the beans with the remaining ingredients and mix gently.
3. Place the bean mixture into a salad bowl or serving tray. Garnish with julienned lettuce and sprinkle chopped red pepper on top.

Approximate cost:

Baked Macaroni-and-Cheese Squares

Ingredients:
- 48 ounces macaroni, cooked 15–20 minutes
- 40 ounces cheddar cheese, shredded
- 8 ounces parmesan cheese, grated
- 2 cups chopped black olives
- 2 cups chopped red pepper
- 1 bunch parsley, chopped
- ? large tomatoes, 2 chopped, ? sliced
- 1 large red onion, chopped
- 3 tablespoons minced garlic
- 4 ounces olive oil
- salt and pepper

- 2 quarts skim milk
- 10 eggs

Preparation:
1. Preheat oven to 375 degrees.
2. Place the macaroni into a large mixing bowl. Add all other ingredients except for the milk, eggs, and sliced tomatoes.
3. In a separate bowl, beat the milk and eggs. Pour in the macaroni mixture and mix well.
4. Grease a deep large baking dish. Pour the macaroni mixture into it. Bake for 50 minutes to an hour and 15 minutes. Approximately 45 minutes into baking, place sliced tomatoes over the top and salt lightly. Continue to bake.
5. Remove the macaroni and cheese from the oven, and let cool. Cut into 2 by 2 1/2–inch squares.

Approximate cost:

Fresh Beet Salad

Ingredients:
- 15 large beets, ends cut off
- 4 tablespoons mustard
- 12 ounces olive oil
- 12 ounces white vinegar
- 4–5 tablespoons sugar
- salt and pepper to taste
- 1 medium onion, julienned
- 1/2 cup parsley
- orange slices, for garnish

Preparation:
1. Boil the beets for approximately 20 minutes. Remove from heat, and cool.
2. Remove the skin from the beets. Cut into halves. Split each half into two wedges.

3. Place the beets in a mixing bowl. Add the mustard, olive oil, vinegar, sugar, salt, and pepper. Add the onion and parsley. Mix well.
4. Place the beet mixture in a salad bowl, and garnish with orange slices.

Tip: Prepare two to three days prior to your event.

Approximate cost:

Dessert: Pear Compote

Ingredients:
- 35 large pears, washed, halved, seeds removed
- 1 quart sugar
- 3–4 cinnamon sticks
- 2 cups raisins
- 1 cup brown sugar
- 2 lemons, halved
- 1 1/2 quarts dry red wine
- 1 orange, sliced, for garnish

Preparation:
1. Cut pear halves into thirds. Place in a large pan, and fill half full with cold water to cover pears.
2. Add the sugar, cinnamon sticks, raisins, brown sugar, and lemons. Bring to a boil. Add the wine. Bring to boil for another two minutes.
3. Remove the pan from the stove, and let cool to room temperature. Pour into a large punch bowl. Chill. Add the orange slices for garnish. Serve with shallow ladle.

Tip: May be prepared three to four days prior. Keep refrigerated.

Approximate cost:

CPSIA information can be obtained
at www.ICGtesting.com
Printed in the USA
FFOW01n0518090217
32211FF